ONE VOICE

THE FIGHT TO SAVE THE CHESTNUT RIDGE

KIM OPATKA-METZGAR

Permission to quote obtained from:
The Indiana Gazette, 899 Water Street, Indiana, PA 15701, for The
Indiana Gazette.

Latrobe Printing and Publishing Co., 1211 Ligoneir St., Latrobe, PA,
15650, for *The Latrobe Bulletin.*

The National Speleological Society, 6001 Pulaski Pike, Huntsville,
Alabama, 35810 for *The NSS News.*

North Coast Media LLC, for *Pit & Quarry* magazine, 1360 East Ninth
Street, Suite 1070, Cleveland, Ohio 44114

Portion of the Jay Reich Bear Cave map © 1993 by J. R. Reich, Jr.,
and the Mid-Atlantic Karst Conservancy, Inc., 137 East Campbell
Street Blairsville, PA 15717. For information on local caves visit
www.karst.org.

Cover background photo by Tim Cairns.

Other source material from:
The Independent, now defunct, was published by Richard Kozar in
Latrobe, Pennsylvania

The Pittsburgh *Post-Gazette*, 34 Boulevard of the Allies, Pittsburgh,
PA 15222 for *The Post-Gazette.*

The Tribune-Review Publishing Company, 622 Cabin Hill Drive,
Greensburg, PA 15601 for *The Tribune-Review, The Blairsville
Dispatch* and *The Ligonier Echo.*

ISBN 978-1512325362

Contents

To all who ever dreamed
of speaking out
for something
they believed in.
Do it with everything you've got.

Chapter 1

The snow crunched. A few days ago it had been powdery. Lighter than a hummingbird's feather. It hissed as your boots broke trail. Today it crunched. It had a crust on it. In the shadowy places you could stand on top of it.

Summer nights, a hike would be glorious. The katydids singing, the crickets adding their chorus. The wind would be cooling, not chilling as it was now. In summer we might have gone farther. But the dam was far enough tonight.

"Come on, Nate." He had his stops, zig-zagging all over the trail. Watering that tree, sniffing at the edge of the fence, shying away from a fallen branch. He always wagged on the descent. The tail didn't go much when the work of the climb began at the old coal drift.

His hair was starting to grow back after the surgery. You could still make out the square patch, but now it had some black in it. He started down, slowing up occasionally so he wouldn't get too far ahead. You could see the dark water through the thinning ice of the reservoir.

Beyond was Chestnut Ridge, the first real view of it to be had from a trail along its base which paralleled the Blairsville Reservoir. You could see it from the roads criss-crossing Derry Township, for miles from the valley below. But to feel it you had to be on her flanks, with her soft, rolling hills looming mysterious. But Nate and I knew her secrets, what lies hidden in that valley. We knew her scars, healed over from decades ago. We knew her new wounds, agape with fresh log skidder tracks. And we knew the plans for her future: to dig deeper, exposing the Mauch Chunk red shales, each lash digging in, getting closer to her core, the faded gray Loyalhanna Limestone which defines her structure, and which conceals her very being—the cold, crisp springs which feed this reservoir—the juices which give life to all that grows in its shadow, and to all who care to

Nate and I on one of our many adventures on Chestnut Ridge.

partake of her offerings.

We stared through the fence which now surrounds the reservoir—"protecting it"—and breathed deeply of her. I needed inspiration, for Nate to recover, and to continue the fight to save her. Whenever I needed inspiration, which was often, sometimes twice or thrice daily, we hit the trail. Only her hardcore lovers would venture out on a day like this, and after three days our sole sets of footprints had carved a narrow gulley through the two walls of snow. It was difficult to stay in it as we carved our way back home. It was either watch the trail and see what kinds of patterns you could make with your lug-soled heel prints, or look around and stumble against the snow wall.

Nate and I knew the trail better than anybody. We knew when a truck had driven over the gravel, whether anybody else had tromped that way. We could even tell what kind of beer they drank—every once in a while finding an unopened one.

It was December, just weeks before the hearing, for our one and only chance to save her. Before we went in the house I turned and breathed deeply once again. I couldn't see her anymore, but needed a last breath of inspiration.

It was back to the computer. I had long ago given up the telephone. When the stories first hit the newspaper we got a lot of ink. Never had an environmental issue gotten such play in the media in Westmoreland County, Pennsylvania, and even in the Pittsburgh media, in decades. Perhaps since the last fight to save her from development.

Chestnut Ridge is one of two prominent ridges in Westmoreland County, the eighth largest county in Pennsylvania. The county lies within the Allegheny Plateaus Physiographic Province, characterized by rolling uplands deeply incised by steep stream valleys. Superficially, the word plateau may seem out of place. However, when compared with central Pennsylvania's Ridge and Valley Province, the Allegheny Plateau's underlying rock formations are relatively flat, with only small undulations and few pronounced folds and faults. Westmoreland County's relatively flat-lying rocks are well exposed along stream valleys and consist primarily of repeating series of coals, clays, siltstones, limestones and sandstones.

The county spans two prominent ridges, Chestnut and Laurel, where upward folded rocks—anticlines—coincide with the topography. The forces of erosion and leveling have acted for a very long time after the Appalachians were folded to form these ridges. The highest parts of these two anticlines correspond with the crests of the Chestnut and Laurel ridges. Those ridges have been heavily eroded, exposing generally older rocks at the highest elevations and successively younger rocks at the lower elevations on their flanks.

The deepest, oldest rocks exposed naturally in the county are found in the water gaps where the Conemaugh River and Loyalhanna Creek incise through the upwardly folded Chestnut Ridge, cutting into its ancient core. The Conemaugh also slices through the Laurel Ridge. All of these water gaps expose the upper portions of Devonian Age strata, over 360 million years old.

It was to this mineral-rich region in western Pennsylvania coal country that settlers slowly migrated. But the land often wasn't available to them, especially in large tracts. During the expansion of non-native settlement of the Commonwealth, land was divided into huge tracts and sold for very low prices. Not surprisingly, it wasn't available to everyone, least of all to those who lived there originally. The wealthy, the well-connected, and those who drew up land acquisitions usually managed to end up with the most and the best parcels.

Land investors offered poor families enticements to settle and clear the land of trees, and, if possible, sign up for a long-term, high-interest purchase agreement on installments. Land acquisition companies, usually comprised of local, state and military officials, conceived the idea of buying up large tracts, making deals with company "settlers" to live on half the acreage, and keeping the other half, so when an area became settled, the company parcels would increase in value. Often the settlers paid around a dollar an acre for their halves. Such companies weren't as successful as their investors anticipated, but many didn't do too badly, either.

A Chester County, Pennsylvania, family came to own much of the Chestnut Ridge in Derry Township, garnering 12 warrants of 400 acres each. The head of the clan, Col. John Hannum, was at various times a member of the Pennsylvania General Assembly, the House of Representatives, and various Chester County offices. He held one parcel, and 11 other family members, named Hannum and Gibbons, owned the others. It's unlikely the family ever viewed the Chestnut Ridge, as its members owned large tracts of land elsewhere. How the family lost the holdings may never be known due to the gap in recorded deeds for these parcels. The most likely theory is that the tracts were sold to a land-holding company, a theory borne out by the next owner, Judge James Wilson, an attorney from Carlisle, a member of the 1787 convention which framed the Federal Constitution and a signer of the Declaration of Independence.

The land then passed to a triumvirate of owners, led by a local iron furnace owner, in the 1830s. Given the need for charcoal for iron furnaces, this more than likely led to the first scarring of the

The Blairsville Reservoir with Chestnut Ridge as a backdrop.

ridge's flanks and the destruction of her old growth forests, her first superficial wounds.

The iron furnace owner, Jacob D. Mathiot, experienced financial difficulties, and much of the land was sold, some to owners of one or two other ridge tracts, the bulk to another local partnership, Anderson and Brown, who carved deeper scars. In search of wealth and riches, local developers began quarrying rock, limestone and sandstone, in small, hand-worked operations, mining stone for house foundations, ballast for the Pennsylvania Railroad running along the base of the ridge, and limestone for agricultural and building purposes. Each subsequent owner took a little more, in hopes for greater gains, but somehow ended up losing it all. Was this the ridge fighting back?

My grandfather moved to Derry Township near the end of this boom time, the first of a large brood sent to work with his father at the local quarry. Too small at age 11 to work in the quarry where his father had gained work, he helped the blacksmith take care of the horses, and often walked with them on some of the very trails Nate and I trod daily. The whole family, 11 children, and other relatives, eventually arrived at their new home at the base of the ridge.

Coal mining upstream of the nearby Borough of Blairsville, about five miles distant, killed off fish in the Conemaugh River and made the water undrinkable, leading to early but unsuccessful efforts to clean up coal mining standards, and to a costly education about the greed associated with industrialization.

This led the borough to search for a new source of water for its residents, in a tiny village at the base of the ridge, called Hillside, the town where my grandfather and his family had moved, where I grew up, and where Nate and I took our daily outings years later.

One of the last acts, ironically, of the small quarry where my grandfather's father worked, was to supply stone for building a dam along a stream called Trout Run, creating a large reservoir and a new source of water for Blairsville Borough.

The large tracts of ridgeland eventually were broken down into smaller parcels, and local residents built small, rough houses, and tried to farm her rocky slopes. These didn't last long, and by the 1920s and 1930s, the few remaining quarry companies became defunct and the small farms abandoned. Some land was acquired by the county for lack of payment of real estate taxes, and the ridge was left to recover from the brief flurry of industry.

This left the ridge for the enjoyment of those who lived in Hillside, Derry, Blairsville, and other nearby towns, to hunt, fish, and explore her natural wonders. Since the 1840s, recreationalists, often on church outings, had visited a large limestone cave about mid-way up the ridge, called Bear Cave. Outings to the cave were written up in local and regional newspapers, and people came to visit, by horseback, canal boat, railroad, and later, by automobile.

Naturally interested in exploring this new vista before him, my grandfather found his way to the cave in the 1920s. His curiosity sparked, exploring caves was one of many outdoor activities he continued to pursue, even into his 70s. He found many caves, took visiting friends and relatives to Bear Cave, and even lowered his companion dog by rope into Rattlesnake Sinkhole to assist him in exploring it.

My grandfather and his brothers developed a deep love for the ridge, and one brother, Donald, came to hold much of the ridge land. My grandfather acquired the Bear Cave and some small parcels of land surrounding it, totaling a little over 230 acres.

By the early 1970s, my great-uncle, Donald Smith, had acquired several thousand acres of ridgeland, but he died in a tragic hunting accident, shot by his son Donald, Jr., who mistook him for a deer.

Albert, my grandfather, continued to document his caving adventures, sometimes with photos, other times with well-versed stories of adventure, passed down to his grandchildren via oral history on his regular Sunday evening visits.

Times being what they were, before Title IX in the 1970s, rough and tumble adventures didn't seem the proper thing for girls, so my sister and I had to sit home and listen to adventure stories told by my cousin when my grandfather showed him the cave. Of course visiting the cave became the only thing we wanted to do.

We came across a book called *Caves of Western Pennsylvania*, read it, saw maps of the caves, and became even more enthralled. This led to our first adventures in the ridge, which just involved finding the things, and later meant venturing in a little ways, but not too far.

This led, on my part, to a love affair, almost an obsession at times, with exploring caves and with the Chestnut Ridge. This led, in turn, to my association with a bunch of crazy cavers and good friends, and to our long battle to protect this beloved ridge. It also led to another kind of battle—family versus family—me, and by affiliation, my family, versus the family of another of my grandfather's brothers, Victor, who came to acquire most of the lands pieced together by his brother Donald after Donald's tragic death.

It led to an eventual effort by three different organizations and many local residents to save the ridge and her pure mountain stream water. It led to the longest case ever brought before the Pennsylvania Environmental Hearing Board over a mining permit. It led to a battle between many ridge lovers—who had each come to know her in our own ways—and development, in the form of big business, big money, and big threats. It led to an incredible series of developments, which are detailed here. It all started with one voice—mine—but that isn't meant to focus on me. It's meant to show those who read these pages that yes, you can make a difference, that maybe, you might come to believe that one voice can meld with many similar voices into a chorus for the common good, and that maybe all it takes is the courage to speak up and the drive to never give up.

Bob Eppley (top) and Carl Trout of Chestnut Ridge Explorers Association working cave digs on the ridge. Eppley's cave "went big."

Chapter 2

The hushed rustle of the young cherry sapling leaves was louder than the trickle of the stream. We were near. The going had been rough and rocky and steep for the last tenth of a mile. The stream had almost disappeared.

"A little more and we should be seeing some outcrop," I huffed. "I guess I'm talking to myself."

Black, panting and dirty, the dog came back.

"Where is he, Nate?"

As the shepherd drank from the suddenly muddy water, I headed toward where the dog had just come from.

"I think we've got something," he said excitedly, never turning around, pitching dirt and rocks wildly up from his already crater-sized hole. I sidestepped a sliding slab of rock.

"Watch where you're tossin' those," I said, to no avail as a small-er rock whizzed through the air. "You almost got the dog."

"We've got a hole. Listen."

Butts in the air, ears to the ground, the smell of wet dog permeating the air, Tom slid a small stone into the crevice.

"Didn't go."

A second one clattered for a few seconds, then there was a plop. Water.

"A-ha!" He held the crowbar skyward.

"Don't get too excited until we get in," I said, taking it from him. "Let me have a go."

As I entered the dig site, Tom pulled a canteen from his pack, which was no easy task since Nate lay on it, biting at flies. Water. We kept getting close, but we couldn't find the way in. There were springs coming out of the hill all over the place, but we were looking for the source, the underground reservoir which fed all of them. We had been cave-hunting—looking for sinkholes along the cave-bearing limestones, for airflow coming out of crevices, for water flowing

9

from cracks, for many years. But now we were doing it with a real sense of urgency.

Most people would think us crazy—maybe even our own families—and most didn't care. But as we looked down off the ridge to the tiny specks of houses in the valley below, I thought that if those people knew what was coming they might care more.

As I took a break Tom reached around to pull the topo map from his pack. Sweat dripped from his nose, his chin, his ears even. It poured through snags in his faded purple t-shirt. He brushed the drip marks away from where he was pointing, but the action only made the creased map damper. The wind was still.

"There is absolutely no surface drainage here at all," he said. "The little spring we followed down here just sinks back into the limestone and where does it go? Where does it go?"

We often used the topo map to reinforce our theories about what lies under the ridge. We had had this conversation often enough, between ourselves and with other cavers.

It was hot in the summer of 1992, and we were running out of time. A little over two years earlier, after I had found my way to a recently-formed local caving group, we had first heard the rumors that my Uncle Victor and his family—four sons—had planned to lease limestone rights to a developer in the hopes of opening a large-scale quarry on Chestnut Ridge. The first company shown the site had thought it unwise—the Loyalhanna Limestone in the Hillside area was not of the same quality as found elsewhere on the ridge, and the springs emanating from it fed the Blairsville Reservoir, a public water supply since the 1920s.

Figuring that it was only a matter of time before another company found the site suitable for them, our rag-tag band of cavers began documenting what we had found there.

A few years before I wouldn't have had the slightest hint of what to do. I was an English major in college, with a minor in art, which involved a lot of time in the studio and the darkroom—my prime interest was photography. I also played college basketball and softball, sports I had played in high school, worked two or three jobs in college, and had a little time for socializing as well. After college, I moved back home to find most of my friends married, with children. I got a job as a staff writer and city editor with the local newspaper, *The Latrobe Bulletin,* where I learned a lot about journalism and how the media works.

It was lonely at home. Even with weekends out with single friends, co-workers and old college friends, there were too many hours to kill. The Chestnut Ridge in my backyard beckoned. I had a lot of pre-conceptions about the ridge, and had always been told that it wasn't safe for a woman to be venturing into the woods alone. I got a dog, Nate, a shepherd-collie-or husky mix, who was just the proper protection.

While I had been away at college my grandfather had established a little parking area on his property in Hillside, about a mile from the Bear Cave, so visitors wouldn't have to park along the road. He thought it would be a good experience for my younger sister, Jackie, and my cousin, Skip, to learn to operate a business, so he began charging $2 per car for cavers to park there. They would chat with people, collect the money and not spend so much "idle" time. Occasionally I helped out too, but once I had a job it was more for the companionship, so Jackie and Skip split the money. Skip lived across from the parking lot, so we would sit in the driveway goofing off while the carloads of weekend cavers came by.

I just happened to be there one Sunday when one particular visitor started to give my sister and cousin a hard time. Knowing him now, I realize he was giving them a hard time in his own, easy-going manner, that he enjoyed the banter. So when he started questioning them about the parking fee, I as much as told him if he didn't like it he could buzz off.

Bob Eppley had quite an amalgam of people in his 4WD listening to all the goings-on, a few older men, and some younger kids, one of whom my sister thought was cute. He slowly, reluctantly, paid his fee. This odd-looking bunch of characters kept coming back, week in and week out, and eventually we looked forward to his giving us a hard time, knowing he was just having a good time.

These were the outings of Eppley's informally-organized crew, called the Chestnut Ridge Explorers Association (CREA). This motley group, which included his children, Rex and Kathy, their friends, Bob's friends, and just about anyone who was interested in coming along, had been exploring and looking for caves in the Chestnut Ridge in Indiana, Westmoreland and Fayette counties since the mid-1970s. Bob had grown up in Johnstown, Pennsylvania, the grandson of a coal miner. He eventually left the area to pursue college and graduate studies, and attended a summer institute in Oak Ridge, Tennessee, which led to an association with a group of "spelunkers"

Firemen on a search for a missing caver who got lost hiking while waiting for friends to exit Copperhead Cave on the ridge. Bob Eppley and I took part in the all-day search.

in 1959. This group introduced Bob to many caves in Tennessee and Kentucky. At West Virginia Wesleyan College in Buckhannon, West Virginia, Bob and other students and faculty members continued to explore caves. Caving was seldom-pursued during graduate school years and subsequent work in New York. But a layoff brought the re-search chemist and his family back to coal country, where he would learn the true extent of the Loyalhanna Limestone and its innards.

Bob, like me, had a copy of the book *Caves of Western Pennsylvania,* and his CREA outings were aimed at exploring all the caves in this book, before they began looking for new caves.

A search and rescue mission for a missing caver on the ridge in the late 1980s caused Bob and I to finally get together. My Uncle Cal (Skip's dad, and my mother's brother), had called Bob when the search began for the girl, since Bob had been going there for some time and knew the ridge quite well. I got involved because of my reporting job, and got to go out with the local firemen and Bob, and search for her. By this time I had acquired an all-terrain vehicle, which gave me more mobility in my explorations on my grandfa-ther's property, and on my Uncle Victor's land. A fireman loaned Bob an ATV, and we were off on the all-night search. The girl turned up unharmed the next morning, and Bob began to look for an ATV to help in lugging digging tools and caving equipment in his explora-tions. As his children pursued other interests, and his other buddies sometimes had other commitments, Bob took me under his wing, and we did a lot of ATV rides looking for Loyalhanna Limestone and more caves.

He showed me all of the local caves, some of them his discoveries, which inspired me to learn more. When we'd drive to a site and take a break, I plied him with incessant questions about all this cave-hunting business. He seemed glad to answer my questions, and in between stops I would think of more questions. It was sort of what you'd call a caving apprenticeship, by a true scientist and master of the local geology and hydrology.

Bob had been involved in the formation of another caving club, the Loyalhanna Grotto, and after putting it off for a while, I finally joined, dashing off a note to the newsletter editor, Tom Metzgar, who seemed to share my interest in local history, and had done a bit of caving, when his work schedule permitted it. On one of Bob's trips to explore a cave Bob had found several years ago, but which was unexplored due to a subsequent access problem (then resolved), Tom was among the cavers on the trip. Immediately attracted to him, I found he had been doing a history of Bear Cave, my grandfather's cave, and from then on we slowly became inseparable. When Bob was incapacitated for a long period due to a severe back injury,

This resurgence below Spider Cave is a wet-weather indication of underground drainage coming from the Loyalhanna Limestone on Chestnut Ridge.

and eventual back surgery, Tom and I, and others from CREA, carried on his work.

Which leads us back to this hot day in the summer of 1992. As members of the Loyalhanna Grotto, Tom and I and other cavers were preparing to try to oppose the quarry my Uncle Victor's family wanted to open. The quarry would mine away the Loyalhanna Limestone, which formed the walls of the caves we were exploring and studying. Without the limestone there would be no caves. From our cave-hunting activities, I had learned that in this particular area, where there is water, there is often limestone, and that most of the springs on the west side of the ridge, in Derry Township, drained into Trout Run, the stream which fed the Blairsville Reservoir.

So we were concerned. If quarrying took away the limestone, and the limestone caves contained large underground streams, which eventually surfaced and emptied into Trout Run, what would this do to the reservoir? Would Blairsville Borough lose its source of water?

When we first heard of the quarry rumor we decided that there wasn't much you could do to combat a rumor. But we knew that scientific data, such as cave maps, documentation of springs, and of the animals that inhabited caves, some of which were listed as a threatened species, might help our cause. So we were busy mapping caves, looking for new caves, which might lead to more knowledge about the underground drainage, and just plain looking, for anything that would help us in our cause.

In 1990 I had prepared a 36-page conservation report, listing much of the data that cavers had gathered over the years on the Hillside area. We quietly circulated it for months, to conservation organizations, officials in the Pennsylvania Department of Environmental Resources (DER), and anyone we thought might be interested in helping us out. Our strategy was to contact conservation organizations, and higher-level governmental agencies, such as on the county and state level. We figured the local board of township supervisors would probably not be able to do anything, since there were no zoning laws in Derry Township, so we didn't bother with them.

I made a lot of telephone calls, and wrote a lot of letters, but no one really seemed that interested in helping protect caves. One Westmoreland County Commissioner, Terry Marolt, thanked me for sending him a copy of our report, and ended his letter with: "Keep up the good work and good luck for all your future endeavors," almost as if he were signing a high school yearbook.

I called officials from the Pennsylvania Game Commission, local and regional environmental groups. All were enthusiastic about our work, but no one really seemed interested in helping.

That led us to come to the eventual conclusion that the only group we could rely on, as a grotto, was the grotto. Which actually was a pretty significant decision, as shown later on in the effort. So we put more time into digging and hiking and exploring. Once we stepped up our efforts to publicize the quarry protest, however, we knew it would only be a matter of time before Uncle Victor denied us permission to go on his land. After all, why would you give free reign to someone opposed to your plans for your land? And the protest was bound to become public soon. So we were getting more frantic, more obsessed with our efforts.

Some of Victor's sons, primarily Scott Smith, an easy-going, outdoorsy-type; and occasionally Oliver, who always enjoyed telling a good story, and even my Uncle Cal often joined Bob Eppley's outings, once the ATV craze hit, and we all had them. Victor, Scott and Oliver, together with Victor's other two sons, Victor Jr., and Terry, had formed the SMT Family Partnership, which was the entity which owned the land, and which was attempting to develop the land. The camaraderie was nice, but in a way things worked against us, because Bob's outings usually involved checking limestone outcrops. So the Smith sons accompanying us began seeing where all of this limestone was, and they weren't interested in caves.

Also adding to the mix was a May 31, 1992, accident in which a teenage girl was severely injured in a cave on Uncle Victor's property, causing a widely-publicized rescue. Rescues are never good for the caving community, as they usually involve inexperienced people with improper gear, and often cause access problems after the rescues are over. Then the victim turned around and sued the owner, which didn't create any more harmonious feelings toward cavers. Although a Cave Protection Act in Pennsylvania eventually helped stay any judgment against the owner, at the time the suit happened, it was widely publicized and didn't help matters at all.

So Tom and I felt it was only a matter of time before we were denied access to the property, and we were urgently looking for anything that would help. That day's dig didn't yield anything big enough for a human to enter, or for that matter, even a dog.

Looking out of the entrance to Hidden River Cave in the mid-1990s, as a stairwell into the cave for tourists was being constructed. It took many years for the cave stream to be clean enough to allow tourists to visit the cave.

Chapter 3

Far, far from Hillside, Pennsylvania—in Kentucky—lies the largest cave in the world, Mammoth Cave, at over 350 miles of mapped passages. There are many entrances over a vast area, most of which are protected by the National Park Service. Not all that far from Mammoth Cave and Cave City lies the town of Horse Cave—that's the actual name of the town. In the middle of the town of Horse Cave is a cave. The cave is not named Horse Cave, however. It is called Hidden River Cave. The cave entrance was once a large dome at the intersection of two underground streams. Natural forces caused the ceiling of the dome to collapse, and created an entrance to the cave. In the 1930s, tourists visited the cave, snaking down a series of over 200 stairs, to the base of the collapse sinkhole to look at the underground rivers and Sunset Dome, a very large room in the cave. Not blessed with formations, one of the cave's attractions was a large population of eyeless cave fish living in the cave's pristine underground river. Tours snaked around a series of pipes installed in the cave in 1887. The pipes came from a ten-inch intake and water was pumped through them to the surface, supplying the whole town of Horse Cave with drinking water. The cave's water continued to be used to supply the town well into the 1920s, even though more people were using wells as their water source. In 1930 there was a drought, so the demand for the cave water increased. In 1931, oil refinery waste was dumped into a sinkhole south of the cave. It appeared in Hidden River Cave.

Several cases of typhoid were attributed to groundwater contamination, leading to a chlorinator being installed in 1932. The town eventually developed another water supply which also served nearby Cave City. Hidden River Cave continued to be a tourist attraction until 1943, when, wrote Julian J. Lewis, "it succumbed from a combination of massive groundwater pollution from creamery waste and declining tourism due to the gas rationing of World War II. ... Until 1964, residential sewage in the Horse Cave area was disposed of through septic fields or outhouses; creamery waste was dumped into sinkholes. In 1964, the situation 'improved' with the construction of the Horse Cave Sewage Treatment Plant. This wastewater treatment plant, located next to Highway 31 about a half-mile south of Hidden River Cave, employed screening, primary sedimentation and trickling filter, secondary treatment. At first a sinkhole behind the plant was used for the effluent discharge, but when it became clogged, two disposal wells were drilled. Both the sinkhole and the disposal wells drained directly into the South Branch of Hidden River Cave. The sewage effluent being dumped wholesale into Hidden River was particularly nutrient-rich and septic due to its high content of creamery waste...A sewage treatment plant nearly identical to the one in Horse Cave was also constructed about five miles south in the town of Cave City. The sewage effluent from the Cave City plant was also released into a sinkhole, this time draining into the East Branch of Hidden River.

"In 1970, the final nail in Hidden River's coffin was driven when a chrome plating plant started operating in Horse Cave. After 1970, about two-thirds of the influent to the treatment plant came from this plant. This sewage was heavily laden with metals, e.g., nickel, chromium, zinc and copper. Levels of these metals were more than adequate to kill the microbes absolutely necessary to the biological operation of the trickling filter units in the sewage treatment plant. Thus, the rock bed of the trickling filter appeared scoured clean. The microbes responsible for breaking down the sewage that would normally cover the rocks in a treatment plant of this type were poisoned by the heavy metals. The metal-laden water was then dumped directly into Hidden River.

"On July 30, 1982, Jim Eckstein and I, at that time biology graduate students at the University of Louisville, entered Hidden River Cave to look at the stream community. What we saw was absolutely sickening. Accustomed to working with the cave faunas of relatively clean streams in nearby Mammoth Cave National Park, what was found was more nearly identical to the polluted surface streams with which we had become so familiar in Louisville. In the South Branch, thick clusters of bright red bloodworms *(Tubifex)* lined the edges of the stream. These worms were able to survive by merit of their red hemoglobin's ability to latch onto the water's rare oxygen molecules. Gray strings of sewage bacteria *(Sphaerotilis)* covered the surfaces of submerged breakdown. The stench in the cave was overpowering. Jim tossed the electrode of a dissolved oxygen meter into the gray water and the readout confirmed that there was almost no oxygen in the water...After returning home to southern Indiana, on the night of August 1, I found myself in the emergency room of Clark County Memorial Hospital deathly ill with a 104° fever. The attending emergency room physician was dismayed as I related to him my trip into the sewage-laden cave two days earlier." (*National Speleological Society News,* July 1993, Pages 208-217).

The story of Hidden River Cave and other environmental tragedies related to groundwater flow and the human impact on it were among the many thoughts that crossed our minds when we heard of the proposed quarry. In 1992, when Tom Metzgar and I attended the annual NSS Convention in Salem, Indiana, we visited both Mammoth Cave and Hidden River Cave. Hidden River was much restored due to the creation of regional wastewater treatment plants that bypassed dumping in underground streams and sinkholes, a solution proposed by the Environmental Protection Agency in the 1980s. An organization called the American Cave Conservation Association (ACCA) was operating a museum and educational facility at the cave. Our minds were full of the hidden impact of human disturbance to groundwater. I had heard rumors of this proposed quarry for a few years. Uncle Victor Smith and his sons obtained the property by a deed dated 1985.

Home from college just a year, I was just beginning to explore the flanks of the ridge closest to Hillside. I was just beginning to know Bob Eppley and his Chestnut Ridge Explorers. At the time I was still learning about caves and what karst was—the topography relating to surface delineations of subsurface features, the sinkholes, drainage patterns, insurgences, resurgences. That's where the Eppley "apprenticeship" came in, and the trips of a thousand questions. What I did know, or sense, was that a quarry above the area that supplied water to the nearby town of Blairsville probably wasn't a good idea. So what do you do about a rumor? That's the question that was brought to me as I attended a monthly meeting of the Loyalhanna Grotto in 1990, a caving club that I'd joined. Grotto members were interested in helping, but what could we do? I pondered that question again and again. The only logical thing I could think of was that we needed information. As a newspaper reporter I was trained to document the facts. I was trained to look at both sides, give each a fair representation, analyze each side, and put into words a story about the event, the meeting, the press conference, the hearing or the trial I had just attended. If there was going to be a quarry, if we were going to try to stop it, if we were going to protect the water supply, we needed facts.

J.R. Reich, Jr. surveying Bear Cave.

Chapter 4

J. R. Reich, Jr. is from Wrightsville, Pennsylvania, on the outskirts of York, not all that far from Harrisburg. He has been involved in caving for many years and edited a book called *Caves of Southeastern Pennsylvania,* composed primarily of descriptions of caves he had explored and/or mapped. Long out of print, most of the caves in that part of the state were either closed, quarried away or already documented. Tom got the idea that someone like Jay might be interested in doing a re-map of Bear Cave, my grandfather's cave. Tom wrote a friend of Jay's, Dale Ibberson of Harrisburg, also a cave history buff, like we were. A few letters changed hands (this was in the days before everyone had e-mail) and soon enough a mapping expedition was arranged. A previous map done by some Pittsburgh Grotto cavers had estimated Bear Cave's length at 3,600 feet. Given that most of the mappers were coming from the York and Harrisburg areas we arranged permission from my grandfather for the cavers to drive up the ridge to the cave and camp near the entrance. My grandfather was thrilled at the prospect of a new map. Jay estimated that with the cave's expected length of 3,600 feet, with numerous crews and three-day expeditions over holiday weekends, it wouldn't take that many trips to re-map the cave. On that day in 1990 I waited in the Bear Cave parking lot for the cavers to arrive. I'd only been in the Loyalhanna Grotto a short time and had no concept of how a cave map was done, but I stood ready with camera and observational skills to note how. The cavers began to arrive at the appointed time and later, on "caver time." Toyota pickups, compact cars, and Jay in a Land Cruiser that looked like it would be more suited to the savannas of Africa or the quicksand and volcanic rocks of Iceland, a place, I later discovered, that was one of Jay's favorites and where the Cruiser had indeed been.

They were prepared for an expedition. Jay, a trim man with glasses, brown hair and a brown mustache, was very much the leader. I tried to stay out of the way as they organized camp and later planned the survey teams. Each team needed three people, but four was better. Jay had segmented portions of the old map and assigned each team a segment to map. Bear Cave is known as a "network maze cave," which essentially means that although the back of the cave is only about 600 feet north of the entrance, there is a lot of passage in between, connecting through crawlways, narrow crevices and duck-unders where the stream runs. These connections were what the surveyors called loops. Inexperienced people who visited the cave without learning proper navigation techniques often wandered in circles and either by dumb luck or the good fortune of running into someone who knew where they were going, managed to wend their way back to the entrances and back down the ridge. Those with less brain power often got it into their heads that they'd spray-paint arrows on the walls to find their way. Only problem was each group painting arrows, their names, and other dimwitted reflections of their half-baked minds had covered much of the walls with meaningless drivel. Some arrows pointed in, some out, some pointed in no obvious way and they all annoyed the hell out of Jay's survey crew.

While it is against the Pennsylvania Cave Protection Act to mark cave walls in any way, small dots with a station number or letter to delineate survey points are permitted. The survey teams found it hard to find spots on the walls of the maze where their stations would be visible as well as re-locatable on the next survey trip. (We then began the massive undertaking of removing this graffiti, a multiyear project).

The excitement of the resurvey was palpable and many members of our Loyalhanna Grotto also showed up to try to help, even though few of us had surveyed before. The camp was set up, the groups organized and things seemed to be going wonderfully—except for one small little critter called the gypsy moth. At its worst infestation ever, these soon-to-be moths were currently consuming the leaves of every oak tree on the ridge, their round, black droppings dripping like rain on the camp, the coolers, the surveyors and the food. Everyone rushed into the cave to get away from being pooped on, exiting only to urinate behind a boulder or a tree near the cave. By the afternoon, everyone was tired, wet, muddy and in a horrible mood. Tired of being crapped upon, by dinnertime many had packed up camp and routed.

Our dreams of a great expedition shattered by moth shit, Tom and I looked at each other and the cave, wondering if the map would ever get done. By the time the Bear Cave mapping was done in 1993 we

Bob Miller, left, and Dale Ibberson surveying in Bear Cave.

were no strangers to lying in a cold, cobble-filled mountain stream patiently holding a mini-mag on a survey station while one of Jay's crew read out compass bearings and clinometer angles measuring slope distance. We were no strangers to holding the end of a survey tape, which had to be painstakingly stretched out between survey stations, the distance in feet and tenths for every point documented by Jay. We had watched other surveyors drop out after showing up long enough to get their names added to the map as helpers. We had learned how to read the instruments, check sketches for Jay, dig connections that the map had shown were near, and crawl into every bloody inch of Bear Cave to see what, if anything, was around the next bend. After three years and three times as many trips as we'd estimated, our re-survey of Bear Cave showed over 8,500 feet of passages, moving it to third on the state's long-cave list at the time the map was completed.

In 1990, as we came to the realization that we needed facts to fight the quarry, we were overwhelmed with the thought of remapping Bear Cave as well as the other caves in the Hillside region. Days melted into weeks, months, and years, and hundreds and hundreds of wet miserable hours. Fortunately, one of the Bear Cave cartographers, Walt Hamm of Pittsburgh, had already begun mapping many of the caves in the Hillside region, especially the larger ones such as Copperhead Cave and Con Cave, just as his hobby. He also began

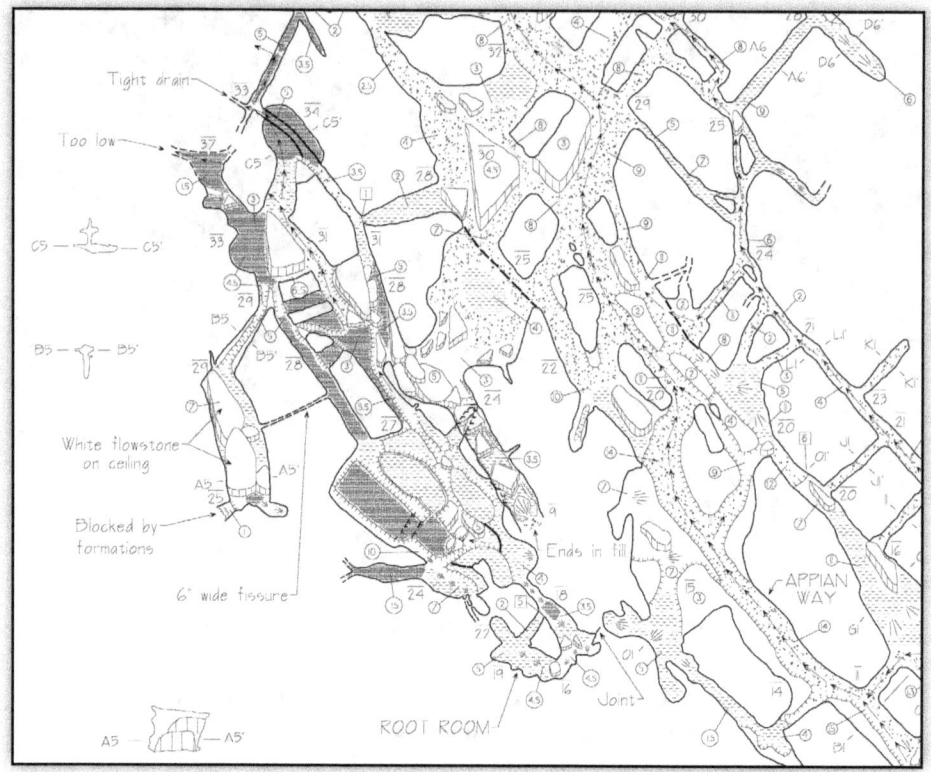

Detail of the Jay Reich Bear Cave map, © 1993.

working on meticulous surface surveys which indicated the relation-
ship of cave passages to each other, surface features such as springs
and rock outcroppings, and the joint patterns of the cave passages.

I helped Walt on a few smaller caves, like Spider Cave, only 57
feet long, and showed him the entrances of other caves that Bob Eppley had taken me to. In January of 1992 I had taken Walt's maps,
Bob Eppley's more recent data and other bits and pieces from various
caving books and newsletters and compiled the 34-page conservation
report I mentioned earlier. Those were our facts, the facts which the
quarry protest would later be based on.

I wrote in the introduction:

"Finding a cave is an uncommon occurrence. Finding several in
one region indicates something about the topography, geology and
hydrology; or, in plainer words, about how the caves are related to
one another and to the terrain.

"In a cave-rich region like Hillside, Westmoreland County, Pa., one
would think the destruction of one cave would not mean anything.

But it does.

"The purpose of this special conservation report is to increase awareness of the caves, cave inhabitants, and the complex underground water systems feeding the Blairsville Reservoir, located above Hillside.

"Members of the Loyalhanna and Pittsburgh grottos of the National Speleological Society contributed to this report, documenting the Hillside area caves through maps, descriptions, and historical references.

"At least two limestone mining companies have expressed interest in the limestone of the region, which could mean every cave but Bear Cave is endangered. But Bear Cave, the most historic and the most-visited, may be affected by mining on adjacent parcels, especially the drainage which keeps the cave active.

"While the Loyalhanna Grotto recognizes the need for limestone mining, and is not, as a whole, opposed to mining, its members are opposed to disturbing this fragile underground.

"The region is a rich habitat for bats, with the Pennsylvania Game Commission doing annual bat counts to keep tabs on the numbers and species of bats in the caves. Copperhead Cave is one of the largest bat hibernacula in the region, and cavers are asked not to visit it while the bats are hibernating. An unusual reptile, the skink, and the threatened Eastern woodrat also live in the cave areas. An activity such as mining would have an extremely adverse impact on these species.

"Finally, grotto members are actively studying the caves in the region, attempting to forge connections with and tie-ins with other caves, either through actual cave fissures or through studies of the underground drainage. The importance of these connections will lie in not only finding new caves, but in finding the source of the water which feeds Trout Run, and the Blairsville Borough Reservoir.

"What has taken millions of years to form, and will take many years of study to understand, could be destroyed in a few short years if mining of limestone is permitted in the area.

"While it isn't a reality yet, it is a possibility. A Somerset-area limestone mining company was interested in the stone a few years ago, sending a representative out to look at the area...While the eventual applicant for a quarrying permit may be neither of these...companies, the fact is, there should not be any quarrying in this region. This is a report on the area, for awareness, for conservation. If it is not taken seriously now, later may be too late."

Cavers were called "rodentophiles" in local news accounts for their desire to protect this threatened species.

Chapter 5

It was a humid hike, warm sweat dripping like we were in a sauna. We were on another hike up the ridge, heading to check limestone and springs on the northern edge of the SMT property and on an adjacent parcel owned by a Millwood resident. An old logging road paralleled the crest of the ridge. In 1992 this road was covered with fallen logs and knee-high grass, which hissed as we silently walked along, dripping, seeds collecting on our jeans. There were three major springs pouring out of cracks in the Loyalhanna Limestone, which were too small to call enterable caves. But the volume of the springs was significant. They trickled across the road, leaving a thick, rich, blackened organic slop that's pungent odor assailed our nostrils. One spring filled what my grandfather called the Frog Pond, and cattails and other signs of wetlands were prevalent.

Hiking from Hillside to the top of the ridge was about a three-hour walk from about 1200 feet elevation to 2300 feet. As usual we had a shovel and a crowbar, camera, and enough food and water to sate our hunger and thirst for a few hours. Tom noticed a piece of blue flagging tape tied to a tree above the limestone outcrop near the first spring. The trail of blue ribbons made our hearts beat a little faster and our pace quicken. There was another, and another, following along the springs, neatly delineating the limestone, clear to the edge of the SMT property line. The soft blue ribbons of plastic tape seemed so freshly tied we half-expected the person who placed them there to come round from behind a tree. I angrily ripped a piece from a tree, stuffing it into my jeans pocket as tangible proof that this plan to mine away Chestnut Ridge was not a figment of my imagination. Tom gave me a sweaty hug. Our find had dampened any enthusiasm we had for cave hunting and we wearily began the trek back down the ridge. The humidity and our discovery drained us of any desire to talk. We knew the time was almost at hand. We had better be ready.

On August 27, 1992, an article appeared in the *Tribune-Review,* the county's largest newspaper, announcing plans for the quarry. It was only eleven paragraphs but the article allowed us to begin to put a face to the anonymous quarryman. Headlined, "Aussie proposes mine in Derry Twp.," the report noted that Clive O. Cutler, from Fox Chapel (near Pittsburgh), was planning the Chestnut Ridge Quarry and intended to apply for permits from the state Department of Environmental Resources to establish a mining operation.

He planned a 25-year operation and wanted to hire between 25 and 30 full-time workers. Cutler listed himself as president of Tasman Resources, Ltd., but did not discuss production goals for fear competitors would use the information against him. He noted in the article that wells would be drilled to supply water and that the mine would work a 65-foot thick seam of limestone on property he was leasing from SMT Family Partnership. His planned underground mine, according to the article, could then be used for other purposes, once mining was completed, such as climate-controlled storage or mushroom mines.

The report noted that Cutler had already briefed Derry Township supervisors about the project and planned to present his plans to county officials.

"I want this to be a showplace," he told the newspaper.

The initial report appeared in the August 27 *Tribune-Review.* The day before the Derry Township supervisors' meeting on September 2, we heard rumors that Cutler would discuss his plans in more detail.

Our time was up. We knew we couldn't let him get up with his promises of jobs and development without expressing our concerns about the environment and the watershed. We knew that every time there was something in the media about the mine we had to counteract it with our own environmental agenda.

We managed, on short notice, to gather a small group of cavers to represent the grotto at this meeting: Tom, myself, father-son duo Paul Damon Sr., and Jr. Dell Bossart, John Chenger and Jim Kennedy, who had done bat studies with the Pennsylvania Game Commission as contract employees, and business owner John L. Long. Paul Sr. had worked with U.S. Steel and was an expert on air quality issues, helping us lend credence to our case, which we determined to keep strictly to the issues. No mudslinging for us, unless, of course, it was in a cave.

So when Cutler, a brash Australian native who once worked in gold mines in South Africa, got up to discuss his plans to mine away our Chestnut Ridge, I almost felt sorry for him, because he had no idea what was coming. He announced plans for a mine to employ between 25 and 30 full-time workers by his Tasman Resources, Ltd., and expressed his hopes that he could help the local economy. He was professional and courteous, and he was also taken by surprise when I stood up to become the first person to voice opposition to his project.

I was 30 years old and had never done anything comparable in my life, although as a newspaper reporter I had covered dozens of controversial municipal meetings. Complicating the matter further was the fact that I was then the editor of the local newspaper, *The Latrobe Bulletin.* Prior to the meeting I informed our staff writer Marie McCandless that I "might say something" at the meeting, but she was to report on it objectively and in as fair a manner as possible. I also took aside our editorial writer, Rich Kozar and told him he could form his own opinion on the issue, which didn't necessarily have to be mine.

The three supervisors at the time were Richard Shaffer, chairman of the board; David Matrunick, and Lon Sinemus. I tape-recorded the meeting and transcribed it later.

One other member of the audience who asked a question was Bev Crocker, who was a member of Residents Advocating Good Environment (RAGE), which was opposed to a proposed landfill in Derry Township, coincidentally, also on land owned by Victor Smith and family of Ligonier.

Introduced by Rich Shaffer, Cutler quickly responded with a "Yes sir. That's the hot seat is it?" and proceeded to introduce himself and his project:

"My name is Clive Cutler. I'm the president and owner of a Pennsylvania Corporation by the name of Tasman Resources Limited. Um, for the last 18 months or so I've been actively researching and exploring for limestone along 10 or 15 miles of Chestnut Ridge. Uh, my research and investigation over the last 18 months led me to the new discovery of a significant reserve of limestone on property in Derry Township, uh, property that's owned by the SMT Family Partnership in Ligonier.

"Uh, my investigations led to uh certain agreements between my corporation and SMT Family Partnership concerning the leasing of a large portion of that property for the purposes of exploring and developing a uh a limestone mine. Uh, the situation as far as I'm concerned, uh, one of my key issues that I've discussed with the uh the Derry Township Supervisors is that there's high unemployment situation in this township. uh, there's a lot of skilled coal mining people and other people who have worked in the extractive industries who are out of a job. And I'm planning to employ 30 to 35 people in full-time employment up in this operation, paying good wages. We're not talking about minimum wage jobs here, we're talking about good paying wages, uh, full-time employment for skilled people.

"Um, the uh, I have spent quite a lot of time with a consulting engineer, uh, preparing a permit application for the mine. The permit application has not yet been submitted to the Pennsylvania Department of Environmental Resources. Uh, and I'm working closely in conjunction with those people, particularly out of the Greensburg office. They are aware of the project. Uh, they conceded to an exploration permit uh back in early 1992, uh, following which there was extensive drilling that I undertook up on the ridge in proving up the resources and making sure that the stone was there. The bulk of the stone lies under the top part of the ridge. As far as the area of mining that I'm particularly concerned in is up on the very high part of the ridge and those of you who are familiar with the uh silhouette outline of the ridge, there's the Bear Radio Tower, there's the Bear Lookout tower, the fire lookout tower, uh, that's about about 2,600 feet elevation above sea level.

"Uh, I intend to mine under that ridge in an underground fashion. Uh, the bulk of this project, which is a long-term project, it will run for 25 years or longer, will be an underground mine. Uh, there will be some surface mining operations obviously, that will lead to an underground mine. It's anticipated at this stage that the bulk of the permit and the bulk of the life for this operation will be from an underground um mining context and uh in as much skilled people out in the community looking for jobs who have worked in coal mines uh I see a good fit.

"I'm particularly concerned about unemployment, I know the supervisors as I've heard them speak about the unemployment problems and they have a lot of pressure on them to try and do something about this situation, and I'm here to tell you that I'm here to hire 30 people as soon as I get the permit I'm in action. Um, that's a brief synopsis of the of the situation. Uh, the supervisors had an opportunity last week we had an opportunity last week to take the supervisors up on this particular piece of property, show them where the initial mining will be done, show them the part of the ridge that's concerned, uh, so they could get an appreciation firsthand looking at the situation up there. O.K."

Bev Crocker asked Cutler who the SMT Family Partnership was, to which he responded: "Uh that's a, the SMT Family Partnership as I understand it is the Vic Smith family from Ligonier. Does that make it a little clearer?"

"That's . . . to do with the dump," she said. "Doesn't he have something to do with that?"

"I might add since you've asked," Cutler said, "my transaction and my agreement with the SMT Family Partnership is an arm's length transaction. The owner of the property has nothing to do with my operations and my plans. He just so happens to have the property with extensive reserves of limestone on it and he happens to be my landlord."

By then Cutler had come across a copy of our cave group's 1992 Conservation Report. With over 70 copies sent to county, DER and other regional and local officials, we had expected this. But we had also come across some early paperwork on Cutler's mine proposal. I first asked him if he was concerned that quarrying would disrupt Blairsville Borough's watershed.

"There's existing dialogue between Blairsville Water Authority and myself and my corporation, uh, these very issues are being ad-dressed between myself and the water authority. I continue to work with the water authority in resolving some of their concerns and I would imagine some of these discussions would continue on into the future," he said.

"Well," I said, "you're concerned about mining on the top of the ridge, but yet your drill holes come down halfway down the ridge which is very much a part of the watershed....So you're just drilling there and you don't intend to mine there? You're just going to spend more money so you can drill down below but you're just going to mine one little area?"

"The mining plans which will be contained in the mining permit application have not been finalized," he admitted. "The mining per-mit that was issued to my company by the Department of Environ-mental Resources covered the whole extent of the lands owned by the SMT Family Partnership.

"Which is how much?" I asked.

"I can't really know that figure," he answered.

"Well you're leasing it from them," I replied. "You don't know?"

"Uh, it's extension? Several thousand acres," he said, expressing a willingness to meet with groups which had concerns to discuss the issues.

I asked him about the name of the quarry, his response being "Chestnut Ridge Quarry."

"It's funny how it's different, different from your report here in which it says Smith Quarry, and I keep reading one thing and you say and/or the documents say another. It says Smith Quarry right here," I said as I held up an early proposal Cutler had filed with DER.

"Is it a crime to change the name of something?," he asked me.

"No," I said. "I understand you said it's 25 years, yet the documents at the courthouse under Tasman Resources says it's a 40-year plan, with 10-year renewable (terms)."

"Um, good, you've done your homework," he said. "Yeah, uh, the success or otherwise of this venture that I'm going into is a function of tons produced and tons sold. I would like to be able to look into my crystal ball and tell you how successful this operation's gonna be. I hope it's truly successful, for the sake of the area and the businesses and the people who are going to be working for me. Uh, they're important issues to me. The life of the operation will be an extent of what the reserves are, what the costs of mining are and whether I can sell sufficient quantities of the product to keep going."

"Yeah, but you seem to estimate that it's only for 25 years and then you have a 40-plus year agreement. You're giving conflicting reports as to what you have on paper," I persisted.

"Miss Opatka, why don't we just agree that it's long-term," he said. "You can devote 25 or 40 years, uh, in 40 years I'll have less hair than I'll have now and in 25 years I'll have less hair again than I have now."

The first paper to report on this was the morning *Tribune-Review.* The headline on the B section read "Opponents of mining plan say rats, caves threatened." Writer Sharon Santus presented Cutler's side as well as the cavers' side. She wrote that "Opatka, editor of the *Latrobe Bulletin*, accused Cutler of distorting his mining plans. She said documents filed at the Westmoreland County Courthouse show a 40-year rather than a 25-year operation with 10-year renewable options."

Jim Kennedy, the Game Commission employee, told Santus the limestone mines would harm the eastern woodrat, a threatened species in Pennsylvania.

Supervisor Rich Shaffer told her he hoped the plan "flies for the sake of the area's unemployed."

The Latrobe Bulletin article noted that the Blairsville Water Authority had recently announced opposition to the mining plan as the authority feared silt from the mine would clog up and damage the authority's new $1.7 million filtration plant, and over time, reduce the holding power of the reservoir.

The cave group's aim, McCandless reported, quoting me, "is preservation. If we let them destroy the rats, bats and the water supply, then find out later we were right, what can we do about it? We can't put them back."

The local *Blairsville Dispatch*, a weekly, came out on September 10 with the headline "Rats! Opponents Won't Cave In To Ridge Mining Plans."

The headlines were giving an early indication that we were not going to have an easy time of it, and that our issues were not the warm, fuzzy issues that the general populace was going to embrace. Rats, bats and caves were not a call to arms for most, but we did have the water supply going for us. And we had scored a few minor hits with Clive Cutler's credibility. It was a start.

Carl Trout of the Chestnut Ridge Explorers Association shows the wear and tear of the "No Trespassing" signs placed on the property of the proposed limestone quarry, effectively closing it to caving.

Chapter 6

The late summer's weather was still hot on that second Friday of September, 1992, when vehicles began to pull in for the Loyalhanna Grotto meeting. As I drove my red Sunbird into a grassy spot near the cemetery, I saw the doors to Saint James Church flung open, welcoming any hint of a breeze. Also known as Yockey's Meetinghouse, this historic hulk of a building was now cared for by the Bell Township Historic Preservation Society, a small group of history buffs from northwestern Westmoreland County. Tom Metzgar was a longtime member and officer of the society, which was chaired by Bill Wolford, coincidentally also chair of the Loyalhanna Grotto.

News of the impending quarry drew a larger than normal crowd to Saint James. Several people were congregated outside a spot where we normally had a bonfire. Paul Damon, Jr., was on the front steps playing a portable video game, and Tom and Bill were inside going over some historical society paperwork.

Bob Eppley had tried to start a grotto in Indiana, Pennsylvania in the 1970s, but not enough National Speleological Society members could be found at the time. Grottos are local chapters of the NSS, which requires the officers be members of the national society, an all-volunteer organization founded in 1941. With a membership of more than 12,000 men and women from diverse backgrounds, age groups and skills, NSS members are dedicated to protecting underground wilderness for future generations. While the NSS is comprised of individual members, in many parts of the country these members have formed grottos or chapters and regional organizations. These groups sponsor trips, offer training, teach and practice cave conservation, and generally provide a framework for enjoying and studying caves.

In lieu of a grotto, in 1978 Bob Eppley began conducting field trips and explorations under the more informal Chestnut Ridge Explorers Association (CREA). After finding and exploring most of the local caves, CREA became focused on digging for new caves and was quite successful. Under Eppley's guidance the small group had doubled the number of known caves in Westmoreland County. Working an area in Yeager Hollow they'd found a number of small caves. The grotto's first chairman, Bill Wolford, had gone on some CREA outings. Eventually it was decided to revive the concept of having a grotto based in Indiana, Pennsylvania again, with meetings to be held at the university there. Bob, Bill and Tom were among the 21 founding members of Loyalhanna Grotto, which was named for the Loyalhanna Limestone prevalent in the area. The group formed in October of 1986 and was officially accepted as a chapter of the NSS in July of 1987.

The grotto and Bob Eppley working as CREA knew the importance of landowner relations, and had designated my Uncle Cal Smith and my grandfather Albert Smith, Bear Cave owners, as honorary members of the new club. So I'd heard of the grotto from my grandfather, uncle and from Bob on his visits to the Bear Cave parking lot.

That winter I attended a presentation by Bob Eppley on caving at the Historical and Genealogical Society of Indiana County. I went with my Uncle Cal and my cousin Scott Smith, one of the SMT Family Partnership Smiths who owned most of the ridgeland. It was the first time I'd set eyes on Tom Metzgar, who edited the club's newsletter. By the spring of 1988 I had joined, ordered the first two back issues from the editor, and continued my weekly outings with Bob, cave hunting.

One day in 1988 Bob took me to a quarry near Hillside where he and the Chestnut Ridge Explorers had discovered a cave around 1980. Shortly after they discovered it, their permission to access the property ended and, respecting the landowner, they didn't go back. Bob had quite a few local contacts and, eight years later, got permission to go back. So he and I went for a drive. We made our way to the entrance and I felt a very strong draft of airflow coming from it. We crawled through a sandy-floored tube, up and over some breakdown blocks, then through a nasty stream crawl that seemed to go on and on and on. We ended in a small dome room where the passage continued. The streamway was blocked by a rock, and a climb to bypass it looked possible, but there were only two of us. At that point Bob told me of the cave's discovery and said, "you're only the fifth person to enter this cave. Ever."

We decided to organize a small group of grotto people to explore the cave and Tom Metzgar was among those in the group. It was August 7, 1988. After the trip we continued our discussion started at the Christmas presentation about Bear Cave and its history. Tom worked a lot of shifts, and as a reporter, I worked mornings into the early afternoon, had afternoons off, then worked a lot of nights and even weekends. We made arrangements to meet and discuss the project at Keystone State Park. Tom brought a box of materials he was ready to give to me. I brought a smaller box of stuff I had compiled. We talked for a few hours. He never gave me the box. I never gave him mine. We decided to share the project of writing a Bear Cave history book, something we're still working on as I write this. For the next two years, due to our work schedules, Tom and I corresponded about a variety of topics, mostly caving. I usually had Mondays off and we began doing research trips to courthouses, libraries and historical societies, and I began borrowing books from his extensive collection of caving materials, learning about caves. By the summer of 1990 we were as inseparable as we could be with our weird work hours.

In 1991, I had written in the grotto newsletter, *The Loyalhanna Troglodyte*, "There is a very real possibility that in the near future a deal could be made which would determine the future (or non-future) of many Hillside area caves, including Con Cave, Copperhead Cave, Rattlesnake Sink, and many other small caves in that area. The deal, which would involve quarrying, might also have an adverse affect on Bear Cave, as far as the stream drying up. Bear Cave itself would not be quarried, as its owners Albert and Cal Smith are not interested in blasting it to pieces. They are also honorary grotto members. But the other caves are owned by less conservation-minded people.

"The Loyalhanna Grotto is planning to protest this...These caves that will be effected or possibly destroyed are in a watershed area, they are the primary drainage for the area, and provide habitat for four threatened or endangered species: bats (including the threatened *Keeni* species), Eastern woodrats, skinks, and rattlesnakes (quarry).

"Much support will be needed. Look for more news in the *Troglodyte* or at meetings as it becomes available. Petition drives and publicity for the cave's plight will probably be part of the game plan, as well as conservation."

Our members remembered that article and the more recent news clips as they gathered on that September evening preparing to enter battle.

Aside from local newspapers affiliating us with "rats and bats" cavers already had bad publicity to contend with, stemming from the May 31, 1992 accident of a Jeannette, Pennsylvania 15-year-old in Con Cave, one of the caves the grotto was fighting to protect. The girl, Mandy Couchenour, had been trying to lower herself into a room called the Rotunda Room from a hole in the top of the dome room when she fell 25 feet. The June 1 edition of *The Latrobe Bulletin* noted that "without special rappelling gear it is not possible to climb down this way." The victim sustained a broken right ankle, bruised her left heel and sprained her hips. A large-scale rescue ensued, requiring over six hours and 100 firemen, as well as cave rescuers trained by the National Cave Rescue Commission.

Not knowing what would happen to the cave after the highly-publicized accident, as well as what would happen to our access once the quarry protest intensified, John Chenger, Keith Christenson, John Long and I videotaped portions of the cave on June 13. A month later, knowing pre-quarry information was crucial, Lee Blazek and Steve Shimatzki began collecting water samples from Bear Cave. On July 26, Dennis Bondi, Rick Page, John Long, John Chenger, myself and Rob Goodman helped videotape Copperhead Cave. Work continued frantically by cave mapper Walt Hamm to map the caves of the Casey Quarry area (which contains Con Cave). John Ciszek, Lee Blazek and I did some video and still photography at Rattlesnake Sink and Doyle's Cave on August 31.

Then, on September 24, 1992, the other shoe dropped. John Chenger, who had been doing much of the data collection with me, and who was our grotto newsletter editor at the time, and I were among those cavers receiving registered letters from my Uncle Victor:

"The SMT Family Partnership are owners of a large tract of posted property along the Chestnut Ridge in Derry, Fairfield and Ligonier Townships. We would like to remind all your members and associate members that this has been, and continues to be posted private property.

"Please advise your members that all trespassers without written permission will be subject to prosecution. Also, please advise your members that all caves on SMT private property have been and continue to be off limits until further notice. Anyone trespassing in and around the caves without written permission will also be subject to prosecution. SMT would ask you to advise all of your members to respect the laws of the Commonwealth of Pennsylvania with respect to private property and we would ask you to respect the wishes of SMT in this matter."

When Bob Eppley, my uncle Cal Smith and I had been going around on Uncle Victor's property with Victor's sons Scott and Oliver, we'd been issued passes from the "Wildlife Club," which SMT had established in order to manage hunting and fishing on the property. Those were now null and void, at least to us, although I kept mine as a souvenir, as I did the Wildlife Club hat Scott Smith had given me. Not one to take banishment lightly, and taking offense at SMT's posting of my late grandfather's property (he died in November of 1991), I wrote back:

"I wish to advise you that Wildlife Club has posted several parcels of land in Derry Township to which it does not hold title, primarily those lands owned by the widow of my grandfather Albert Smith. I would like to remind you of this, and note that I and members of the organizations to which I belong will continue to use this property which Wildlife Club has posted and does not own or pay taxes on. (This also includes my yard, which was posted with a Wildlife Club poster last year.)

"I also advise you and any members of SMT Family Partnership to respect the laws of the Commonwealth of Pennsylvania with respect to private property which the SMT Family Partnership, its individual members, and Wildlife Club does not own, and subsequent posters and survey markers which may be along those lines. In addition, I wish to advise you to respect any and all rights of way which go with your late brother's properties and are not owned or shared by you, members of SMT Family Partnership and/or Wildlife Club. I will continue to use such rights of way as long as I or persons who have given me permission to do so continue in this manner.

"Copies of your letter to me have been sent to the newsletter editors of both the Pittsburgh Grotto newsletter and the Loyalhanna Grotto newsletter. Such advisories will also be issued to any other groups you deem necessary..."

My grandfather might have been gone, but his temperament and spirit had been so ingrained in me that my parents jokingly called me "little Albert."

Our access to the property banned, our focus shifted to paperwork, as well as continuing data collection and cave mapping on adjoining parcels which we still had access to. It was an interesting fall.

Vandals spray-painted the entrance area of Con Cave, which the owners quickly gated to deny cavers access.

Chapter 7

K.D.M. Big, blue, bold, bright. Painted on the quarry face above the Con Cave entrance. The date was painted, too. 3-9-91. He must have been pleased. His initials were now much larger and brighter and fresher than anyone else's.

Like the catastrophic failure of a burst water pipe or the sudden explosion of a tire's sidewall from a rock shard at highway's edge, the anger welled up faster and burst out with more potency than the burn from a rattlesnake's strike. Pressure forced the furnace door open and there were white-hot embers baking amid the low rumble of flames hard at work.

I don't remember what I said, and most of it would probably not bear repeating. Twenty different synonyms for moron came to mind with enough adjectives to fill a grocery cart.

"Hope they didn't get Bear, too."

It was an innocent enough remark, but our boots seemed to sprout wings and quickly we were up and over the hill to Bear Cave. There were a bunch of rough-looking cavers in the entrance area of the cave, and yes, they said, "K.D.M." had been there, too.

It happened again in July of 1991, only a summer camp group caught the perpetrators. It happened to be a Monday, my day off, and I quickly videotaped the spray-painters in the Bear Cave parking lot, as well as the camp group kids' testimony.

In the spring of 1992 our anger at the painting turned to happiness with two successful prosecutions, the first two in Pennsylvania under the state's new cave protection law. As a result, Loyalhanna Grotto received some reward money from the National Cave Vandalism Deterrence Committee. We split half of the second reward money with the camp group. The rest was used to build our war chest to fight the quarry. With a $500 grant from the Richmond Area Speleological Society and $1500 in reward money, the $2000 in our treasury was what we had to oppose a proposed multi-million dollar operation.

Anger, however, wasn't limited to our feelings toward vandals.

Some members of the caving community, not perceiving the quarry as any real threat to the caves, weren't happy with the closure of the SMT Property. Then there were the spelunkers, a derogatory term (at least to cavers) referring to "flashlight cavers," or people who cave with no helmets, one or fewer lights per person, without proper clothing and footwear. Oftentimes, we joked, their backup lights were "Bud Light" and "Coors Light." These spelunkers, as well as some organized cavers, for a time continued to access the property, which of course, SMT played to the hilt in its defense of its private property rights. The media barrage was wearing on us. But it was also wearing on SMT.

After I sent my letter to Uncle Victor, his son, Vic Jr. responded a few days later, on October 1, noting that "if anyone desires to control SMT land they should make a serious offer to purchase the land...Continuing to use the news media to create unwarranted and unjustified public concern over private property issues will gain you or your group nothing."

The following day the *Tribune-Review* published an editorial endorsing Tasman's efforts to quarry away the ridge, again taking a jab at the caving community's efforts to protect the bats and woodrats.

Loyalhanna Grotto members did Adopt-a-Highway for eight years along Route 217 in Hillside, so the accusation by Vic Smith, Jr., of cavers as litterbugs angered many of the club's members.

Copperhead Cave was also gated with a rebar gate that was not bat-friendly, meaning the spaces on the bar forced bats to land on the gate in order to exit the cave, thus exposing them to predation.

The newspaper reported Victor Smith had a cockeyed idea that he could do what he wanted with his own property. The editorial stated that the people would then start to think they could do what they want with their own money. It surmised that cavers were made because the caves were closed, and said that unless there was "irrefutable evidence" that environmental damage would occur, "the DER (Department of Environmental Resources) should endorse it."

The newspaper reported that Smith should be able to make money from use of his property as long as it did not harm its human neighbors, and lauded Cutler's statement that 30 jobs would be created. It concluded by noting that it was good news, even though it would be of little comfort for the "rodentophiles in our midst."

Around the same time the girl who had been injured in the Con Cave accident in the spring filed suit against SMT Family Partnership. The suit, given the issue of caves and the quarry, received media attention in full, with members of the Smith family continuing to take jabs at cavers, and allowing themselves some redemption for closing the caves. In the September 29, 1992, edition of the *Tribune-Review,* Vic Smith Jr. commented on the publicity that had resulted from cave accidents and lawsuits, stating that was the reason for the

The entrance to Rattlesnake Sink before, and, at right, after the owners filled it with logs and debris.

cave closures.

"The point is," Smith said, "this is private property and these people are trespassing. They come up here and litter and destroy the roads. We're tired of it."

Our protests as well as some cavers who had not respected the property's closure incurred the wrath of SMT and Tasman. Gates with no doors were placed on the two most popular caves, Con Cave and Copperhead Cave. Rattlesnake Sink was filled with logs. Trees were cut all around the entrance areas of Ken's Cave and Hillside Bone Cave. Hillside Run Cave was filled with dirt and logs. All the caves on the property that the Smiths could find were physically closed. That stopped the spelunkers, as well as cavers who insisted on continuing to visit the property. There were actually two good things arising from the physical closures: the first was that it stopped the trespassing, so that ammunition could no longer be used against us; the second was that "an anonymous contributor" had provided grotto newsletter editor John Chenger with photos of the cave gates, which were not "bat-friendly," meaning the spacing on the grid of rebar was not of the correct dimensions to allow bats to fly through the holes.

If the Smiths wanted to use the media against cavers, we decided we weren't going to take it lightly. The war of words had begun in earnest. We planned a press conference the following weekend, meeting at the Bear Cave parking lot. If we couldn't enter Uncle Vic-

tor's property, at least we could look at the ridge from there. If the media wanted "sound bytes" and "quotable quotes" they were going to get them.

I, as editor of the daily paper most local to the site, had to be careful not to present my personal bias in *The Bulletin*. My reporters and editorial writer were instructed only to write articles from sources other than cavers, although several cavers wrote "Letters to the Editor." That meant our coverage consisted minimally of what the Blairsville Water Authority was doing to protect its watershed, and of what transpired at public meetings which our staff covered. *The Bulletin* did not cover the caver press conference, but at least one television station did, as well as the *Tribune-Review* and *The Blairsville Dispatch,* a local weekly. I tried to stay out of the limelight.

In response to Vic Smith Jr.'s statement about cavers destroying SMT's roads, Tom Metzgar retorted, "We're destroying roads in our lug-soled boots while they're riding around up there on bulldozers?" Tom was interviewed for the television program, and Loyalhanna Grotto Chairman Bill Wolford spoke on the geology of the ridge, explaining how the watershed could be disrupted.

We made the front page of the Sunday *Tribune-Review* on October 11. Try as I might to stay out of the limelight, there were times when I just couldn't help myself, as noted in the pullout quotes which had me saying things like "We're going to fight this thing until the caves die or we do."

Writer Sharon Santus had covered our press conference, which focused on the improper gating of the caves and thus the disruption of the bat habitat, and our announcement that we would hire an attorney to press our case. Clive Cutler, the Tasman Resources CEO, responded, noting "they can hire all the attorneys they want ... I can give them a list." Jeff Himler reported in *The Dispatch* that Cutler said he would apply for the mining permit within six months and was "continuing to consult with the Blairsville Water Authority."

Cutler, quickly realizing he had to work with the agencies involved, noted to Santus that he had been working with the Pennsylvania Game Commission and the DER to ensure his operation would be environmentally sound, and said none of the caves would be quarried away. He came out on October 20, 1992, in the *Tribune-Review* saying "spelunkers a threat to welfare of bats," as the headline read. He also added "if there was a chance the reservoir would go down or disappear I wouldn't want to do this project." The Blairsville paper, which is owned by the *Tribune-Review,* reprinted the October 20 article by Paul Pierce with a different headline two days later, noting that "Developer Says Opposition Group has Bats in Belfry."

Then began the barrage of letters. I began writing to prominent members of the caving community seeking support, such as then-president of the National Speleological Society Jeanne Gurnee. She responded a few days later, noting that the newspaper editorial "Whose Land Is It?" covers the biggest problem. "But when development involves endangering aquifers, species and other resources, environmental and municipal authorities should act."

In the meantime, Indiana County's largest newspaper, the *Indiana Gazette,* began covering the fray. Bill Graff, an assistant editor who frequently wrote about Blairsville Municipal Authority meetings, reported on September 19 that "Blairsville is now complying with two costly state Department of Environmental Resources orders, which will cost the taxpayers and water and sewer customers in Blairsville $7.1 million in construction costs. Can't DER also protect Bairdstown and Blairsville-area residents from a lowly dump and dust-making rock quarry?" Graff began tying in SMT with a garbage dump proposal just outside of Blairsville. SMT had agreed to allow a landfill on its property there, a very unpopular notion that had already rankled Blairsville residents. Tying the dump and the quarry together, as Graff did without our encouragement, returned SMT's jabs at us with a good solid blow.

I wrote an article for the October-November 1992 *Sylvanian,* the statewide newsletter of the Sierra Club chapters in Pennsylvania, noting "Quarrying Threatens Groundwater."

Cavers also did a good job of speaking for themselves. Lisa Hall's "Letter to the Editor" appeared in the November 8, 1992, *Tribune-Review*. She noted that "cavers are speaking for something which cannot defend itself. They are carrying out the important task of informing the public. It keeps the opposition on its toes, makes them stick to the guidelines and follow the rules."

John Chenger wrote a letter refuting claims by Vic Smith Jr. that cavers were litterbugs, citing the Loyalhanna Grotto's Adopt-a-Highway Project in Hillside, where members picked up trash along a two-mile stretch of highway four times a year for eight years..

Tom Metzgar wrote that the "Smiths are poor stewards of the land if they deprive future generations of these unique and irreplaceable natural features."

Caver Rob Goodman in Copperhead Cave.

Chapter 8

Round, white discs of paper burst out of the overflowing three-hole punch and onto the carpet below the desk. They poured onto manila file folders, heaps of originals, heaps of copies, heaps of caving publications, heaps of watershed articles, and a growing heap of newspaper clippings of our quarry protest. There was no vacuuming them up as there was no room for a nozzle attached to the hose let alone the whole vacuum cleaner.

We were glad to have had the grant money when we discovered the cost of the copies of Tasman's preliminary paperwork filed in the DEP District Mining Office in southwest Greensburg. John Long was among the cavers who offered to put his copy machine to use duplicating our copies of the original paperwork. I was attempting to organize the copies and get them into the hands of people who would be able to make good use of them.

Our fieldwork temporarily at a halt, except for friendlier properties, the paperwork seemed to reproduce as quickly as various rumors sprouted about Chestnut Ridge.

My January 1992 Conservation Report on caves of the ridge was now ancient history. SMT had used it as a guide to fill in cave entrances. DEP had copies. It had served its purpose.

At the same time we were undertaking our quarry protest there was another one going on in central Pennsylvania. Nittany Grotto, a student caving club affiliated with Penn State University, as well as with the NSS, was among the groups seeking to prevent expansion of an existing limestone mine in Bellefonte, and destruction of a cave called Hosterman's Pit.

One of the main thrusts of Nittany Grotto's fight was a state regulation allowing the land to be declared unsuitable for mining. The UFM designation would prohibit surface mining in areas where it could affect fragile or historic lands or result in significant damage to important scientific or aesthetic values or natural systems. A push was underway to amend the UFM regulations to eliminate the state's regulatory authority over non-coal lands. That meant that the UFM designation would not apply to proposed limestone quarries.

Given the depth of the arguments, which would eventually be brought before the state's Environmental Hearing Board, we wrote letters in support of Nittany's efforts; but we couldn't afford to put all our eggs in one basket. Thus, we left the UFM fight up to Nittany and the many other groups supporting the designation for non-coal lands, and continued collecting our own data.

Time seemed to go by quickly, though.

All the attention occasionally got us invited to tell local groups about our efforts. Tom Metzgar had been involved in innumerable organizations over the years, historical societies, caving groups, and a wide range in between. He'd served on the boards of directors of many of them, various committees, and certainly knew how to liaison with people. His parents were both schoolteachers. His maternal grandfather had been a coal strip miner and tree nursery operator, while his paternal grandfather had been involved in education and had concluded his career as superintendent of the Greensburg Salem School District, with an elementary school in New Alexandria named for him. Additionally, in Tom's job as a safety and security supervisor for PPG Industries (via Cauley Detective Agency's contract for service), he knew how to work with people.

On the other hand, my examples had been my hot-headed, stubborn, forthright grandfather, and various editors at *The Latrobe Bulletin*.

Vince Quatrini was a local legend. Finishing his career as editorial editor of the *Bulletin*, there was absolutely NO getting the last word in on Vince. Pity the local politician that didn't quite see things the same way Vince did. As we said, and as Vince often wrote, things didn't always "auger well" for them. Vince could come up with some jewels, although to the opposition they were more like cubic zirconia. Late mornings, just before deadline, in the newsroom he would emerge from his cubicle, a long typewritten missive on rolled paper (back before the computer era had reached us). Whoever had attended the previous night's municipal meeting with him got to read the thing to make sure he was right on all the facts. Local politicians often spent the mornings after meetings on the phone in loud arguments which Vince, who, of course, always won.

Then there was Bill Costanzo, or "Noz," as we called him. The feisty editor was another newsman with ink in his blood. He was very protective of his staff, and, right or wrong, like Vince, defended the *Bulletin* and its writers to the last drop of argument. Both had retired, thus elevating me, the city editor, to editor, to carry on their legacy, which probably served me better in the quarry protest than it did in the news industry.

For a brief stint after college I had spent a year working in the payroll department of a trucking company. But I didn't learn to swear like a trucker until I worked in the newsroom of *The Latrobe Bulletin.*

In January of 1993 it had been not quite a half-year since the SMT property was closed. But the interest in the quarry protest was still strong.

Tom had been approached by the local Forbes Trail Chapter of Trout Unlimited and asked to speak about the protest at one of the group's meetings, held at the Touchdown Club along Route 30 in Unity Township. He invited me along to help with the exhibits. I was glad to go, especially since I didn't have to do anything but sit there and listen to him. We loaded up a bunch of photo albums showing the caves, streams, springs and critters we'd found and photographed on the ridge. The room was full of trout fishermen. During their regular meeting they'd exchange ties and talk about various projects, much like a cave club meeting, only the focus here was on fish, as well as the streams they lived in.

We were invited because the group was interested in learning how the water quality of Trout Run and the Blairsville Reservoir would be affected by the mine.

Tom gave a good talk at meeting's end, and was doing quite well in a friendly question and answer session. He had cultivated quite a slew of interested anglers. Then, to the surprise of Tom, the club members and me, one man at a table questioned the legitimacy of the protest. In polite respectfulness, none of the club members said anything. The man looked familiar to me, but I couldn't quite place him as I angrily sized him up. Tom was nearly speechless, not because the man had questioned him, but because he had just finished carefully explaining in great detail all the potential affects. There was a drink on the table and Tom might have been assessing how many the man had had, or he might have been trying to come up with a politically correct answer.

The Costanzo, Quatrini and Albert Smith in me all seemed to merge into one and after a few minutes of silence in a crowded room full of people, I thought that if Tom wasn't going to respond I would. Aside from the waitresses, I think I was the only woman in attendance. Suddenly all eyes were on me, including Tom's, as I strode over to our exhibit table and pointed out our documentation of all the various things that Tom had just stated. When the man refused to get up and look at them I grabbed a photo album and took the pictures to his table, jabbing at pictures in the book with my index finger.

When I was done, the chairman of the group asked meekly, "any more questions?" and made haste to quickly end the meeting turned potential minefield. Many people quickly exited, although some of the officers took the time to thank Tom for coming out to talk to them. I don't think anyone thanked me. But I puzzled over that man's identity for a long time. Then one day, it hit me, that it was Dan Slavek, Jr., owner of a local construction firm, Derry Construction. He knew my grandfather and I'm sure my Uncle Victor. I speculated as to why he had such a strong interest in seeing the quarry through, but had no answers for that one, not even a picture in an album to show anyone. (It would be several years later, but the question of Slavek's interest in the quarry would become abundantly clear. I just didn't know it then.)

I decided the public speaking route wasn't my cup of tea and although Tom teased me about my passionate outburst later, I worried that I might end up being a hindrance to the cause.

That same month, the Blairsville Water Authority's consultant had presented an informational session on the watershed. James Casselberry was a hydrogeologist who spoke our language. Water authority members as well as members of Blairsville Borough Council were in attendance.

While Casselberry was careful not to take sides—or, as I thought later—to reveal too much of his case for Blairsville, enough data was gleaned from an expert not affiliated with cavers to give us unbiased hope for success.

Casselberry had previously supervised the drilling of two wells for the borough to supplement its water system. One was above the reservoir, right along Trout Run, and the other was below the spillway of the dam. The well below the dam was in the Pottsville sandstone, had a high iron content, and its water had to be treated before use. The one above the dam was 390 feet deep in a "fracture" in the Loyalhanna Limestone, the same cave-bearing limestone we were interested in. The water, Casselberry said, was so pure it did not need treatment.

"The rocks which supply the bulk of the water to both are the rocks which outcrop along the ridge crest," Casselberry said. "And these are the areas which must be looked at. The rock water which feeds the upstream well is the very rock they are going to mine."

Bingo! Strike three! He shoots and scores! This was exactly what we knew and needed to hear from someone else.

Clive Cutler had hired C.G. Walton to do a report on the watershed in response to our first conservation report. Walton dismissed the limestone as an aquifer, reporting most of the water was held in the Burgoon sandstone. Later, Cutler hired a hydrogeologist, Dr. Richard Parizek of Penn State University. Just a month earlier Jim Casselberry had had a meeting with Cutler, Walton and Parizek. Not surprisingly, he was not able to glean all that much information from them, since the direction the protest was taking would put them all on a course to clash, head-on, at some point.

But we learned, for the first time, at the informational session, the areas Cutler planned to mine:

—The spur under the Bear Cave Fire Tower, which would be deep mined.

—The spur to the north of a meadow on top of the ridge, out of which emanated the three springs that eventually feed the Bear Cave stream. This area would be stripmined.

—The limestone surrounding and containing Copperhead Cave, which would be stripmined.

Casselberry said he felt that due to the negative affect of their first report, they were unwilling to provide any precise mining plan, no description of how long or how fast the area would be mined. But he said they did look at the map and give a basic description of where the mining operation would be.

The watershed area upstream of the reservoir is approximately 1,530 acres. About 150 acres, or one-tenth of the watershed area, would be mined initially. The closest mining would be 4,800 feet up the valley. Casselberry was told the access for quarry trucks would not occur in the watershed.

He said that water is recharged along the Trout Run stream valley and the flow is concentrated in fractures and solution conduits. "There is a lot of water there, in intensely fractured Loyalhanna."

The concern, he said, which was the same as ours, was that mining would somehow interrupt these fractures. If the major fracture zones run up toward the quarry, there would be potential avenues for groundwater flow to be affected if the conduits were intercepted and mined away by the quarry.

"If a major fracture intersects the mine site, we may be able to tell them not to do it," Casselberry said. He said they were calling a "unique feature" on the ridge "the Needle." This was a fracture they said was about 2,500 feet long in the area they planned to stripmine. It was "straight as an arrow," he added. What they really meant, we thought, was Copperhead Cave, which is nearer to 4,000 feet long.

Other issues also came to light, such as a replacement source for the Blairsville reservoir if the watershed was disrupted, substance control for blasting powder and fuels, the potential for contamination, turbidity from sedimentation ponds, and more.

Then he estimated that the quarrying would net a half million square feet of limestone per acre, 40 percent of which has to stay in place if there is deep mining. That, Casselberry said, would amount to a profit of about $1,050, 000 an acre.

The Smiths had begun actively logging the ridge in the area of the proposed mine; after all, there could be no trees in a stripmine. While we couldn't see the damage up close, we could see the gashes and log skidder roads, and the silhouette of earth, not trees, at the top of the ridge under the fire tower. They had plans for that property, and, at $1,050,000 an acre, we were not about to stop them.

Casselberry added that the DEP had been "zero" effective in controlling sedimentation and assuring the Smiths followed all the rules with their logging operation. At that rate, the water authority would have to have an inspector on site weekly, or at the very least, every other week. With increased water turbidity, as the authority was experiencing due to the logging, the borough would have to factor in more chemicals, more testing and more water treatment if a mine were to go in. Costs were adding up on both sides, millions of dollars. We had spent a few hundred of our $2,000.

Chapter 9

The pavilion was crowded as the awards ceremony wound down. After three days of caving, partying, "speleo-olympics," river sports and camaraderie, the weekend was coming to an end.

Every Labor Day weekend for decades a group of cavers has gathered in West Virginia for a reunion. It's called the Old-Timers' Reunion or OTR. There are vendors of caving gear set up on a vendor's row, live music, disc jockeys, tent cities of caving clubs from all over the southern, eastern, and central United States. Tom and I had been going for a few years, one of our chances to explore some of the well-known West Virginia cave systems, and to meet and socialize with other cavers.

That OTR we went with a purpose—our cohorts from Loyalhanna Grotto had paperwork to shuffle. Since it was my idea, I was delegated to get up on the stage in front of the large crowd watching the awards, and give a plug for our quarry protest. Our objective was to get as many cavers as we could to sign petitions that we would then submit to the Department of Environmental Resources to help our cause. Remembering the fiasco with Trout Unlimited, I wasn't worried about the reception I'd receive in the caver crowd. We had our team ready, with a few reams of paper on which were printed our petitions, two to a sheet. We had lots of pens, and lots of volunteers to circulate through the pavilion.

I stepped up to the microphone, said my part, and then helped the crew get to work. When it was all said and done we had gathered five hundred and ninety six signatures from members of the caving community and other environmental organizations from 13 states, Canada and England.

Our other mission for the weekend was to meet with a caver named John "Chuck" Hempel. Chuck began his caving career with the Pittsburgh Grotto as a teenager visiting many of the caves of the Hillside area. He moved on to bigger and better things in West

Virginia and lives in Dailey, across from the OTR site. He is an environmental consultant, having studied at West Virginia University, and has his own consulting company, EEI/GEO. More often than not, up to that time, he had consulted for people wanting to put in coal and limestone mines, offering his expertise to ensure the least amount of impact to the environment.

Chuck often volunteered for security at OTR, and that year we caught up with him in between calls. He wasn't that tall, but his experience in working with cave rescue, as well as his service in the military, left him with an air of authority, of command, of confidence that was at times intimidating, at other times comforting.

The OTR event is put on by caver volunteers, much as all caving events are. Unless someone works as a guide in a commercial cave, in an earth science such as geology, or at a university doing teaching and research into cave and karst issues, there aren't many cavers who make a living off their favorite past-time. That suits many of us just fine. After a few summers working in an amusement park, where I had to be there six days a week for twelve hours a day, I rarely visit them now. I certainly don't want to feel that way about caving, like it's something I have to do. The spontaneity, the enticement of being the first person to find and explore a passage and the sense of adventure are not something I can find in the aboveground world.

Often cavers who work in unrelated fields have a surprising amount of expertise in the science of speleology. The other good thing about the caving community, since we're mostly comprised of volunteers, is that cavers are more than willing to help each other out, usually for nothing more than the time it takes to complete a project.

Chuck had a personal interest in the caves of the Chestnut Ridge at Hillside—these were among the first caves he had explored, the caves that had opened up a whole world of wonder to him. He was offering his services to us at no charge—all we had to do was pay for his expenses, such as copying costs, display costs, and map reproduction costs. But we had our mostly untouched war chest of $2,000 for that. It wasn't just a "David and Goliath" situation—in the eyes of Tasman Resources and their engineers and experts, it was a joke.

In August of 1992 Tasman had hired C.G. Walton of Clarion, consulting geologist, to refute our concerns about the potential effects of proposed mining of the Loyalhanna Limestone on water quality and quantity in the Blairsville Reservoir.

"Various press releases and conservation reports generated by regional speleological societies and their individual members have taken strongly adversarial positions toward any mining in the area. These have made definitive statements about the perceived threat that mining would pose to the water supply for the town of Blairsville, more specifically to the Blairsville reservoir which is located in the drainage channel of Trout Run downstream of proposed mining area.

"...In general circumspection, it should be apparent that most of the many pages of description and mapping that have been published about the caves of the area over the past century and a half would have been impossible without use of SCUBA gear or air lines if the caves truly contained large quantities of standing or flowing water."

The report was an attempt to intimidate us with technical detail, implying that we didn't have the expertise to deal with them on the same level. Chuck Hempel changed that—only we were saving that tidbit of information for the most appropriate time. No sense launching a cannonball until we were sure to make a hit.

At the time of our OTR petition drive, in September of 1994, it was almost two years since Clive Cutler had said he would file his permit application. In anticipation that the time was near for the application to be filed, we published our third conservation report.

I wrote that "this does not mean that we should forget the caves. ... It's been two years since cavers were notified they were not welcome on the property. We have not been able to monitor the caves, or the effects of the closings and gatings. We don't know what is going on with the species that inhabit the caves.

"What we do have, however, is a wealth of data on the caves of the Hillside area, which have been known and studied for many years....

"The first conservation report, which I edited, attempted to pull together much of the data on the caves, with maps, and other geologic, biologic and hydrologic information.... The second report, which John Chenger edited, was our attempt to respond to many of the allegations and accusations made against cavers once the media got wind of the protest, and Cutler and SMT began fighting back.

"This report focuses on two things, the Blairsville Water Authority's watershed and the Bear Cave...While SMT does not own the Bear Cave, the cave could very well be affected by mining. So while the SMT property has been closed, grotto members have been focusing on the property that we still have access to. We have done water quality assessments and put to rest the speculation about where the Bear Cave's stream flows. It enters the Shirey Run Watershed.

"...We have only scratched the surface as to the affect of mining on the ridge above Bear Cave could have, however. We've just started studies on the aquatic life in the Bear Cave stream. And once the water exits the cave we have Shirey Run. We haven't begun to look at what kind of affect mining would have...While the lower dam at Shirey Run is no longer used for a water supply for Torrance State Hospital, the upper dam still is. Native brook trout still populate the stream, and the water quality (is excellent).

"We're at the waiting stage right now. We have been for some time. During that time we've begun to get our experts lined up: Chuck Hempel is leading the way. Helping him out will be Eb Werner from West Virginia University. We've contacted many other conservationists, cavers, and others willing to offer their expertise and help.

"We're not very vocal right now, which suits us just fine, but that will probably change. When, we don't know.

"The important thing right now is that we can't forget. We can't go to most of the caves which are in jeopardy now, but even if we could, it doesn't change the fact that they are threatened. If you've been there, remember. If you haven't, hopefully our efforts will save the caves and you may have a chance to see them someday. Or your kids might. Or your grandkids.

"Right now we need you to keep thinking about those caves. Be ready to fight for them. Support our efforts by buying a Save the Caves t-shirt...Think about what a terrible tragedy it would be to lose the (caves), not just for a few years, but forever."

Shortly after our third conservation report was published, the other shoe dropped. The last advertisement for the mining permit application appeared in *The Latrobe Bulletin* on Thursday, October 13, 1994. Following that ad there was a 30-day comment period during which we could comment on the application.

We obtained a complete copy of the permit application, at a cost of $140. The fight was on. Written comments were due November 13, 1994. We intended to request a hearing, at which time we would launch cannonball Hempel. But there was a lot of preparation and so little time, now that we had the actual proposal, the permit application, their plan of action.

Chapter 10

I pulled into the little patch of a stone parking area with patches of grass springing up between the rocks. The grass in the yard had gone to seed and there was no skirting at the bottom of the mobile home. My tennis shoes crunched on the little stone walkway wending its way through the calf-deep grass. Two steps to the small four-by-eight foot platform that served as a porch and I knocked on the door. It was slightly ajar in an attempt to ventilate the kitchen area where Tom sat at the round kitchen table filled with stacks of paper. He was waiting for me.

I surveyed the kitchen. There appeared to be a mail stack, a book catalogue stack, various piles of newspaper clippings sorted into the cardboard flats that had once housed two dozen cans of beer of some sort. There was a case of Stoney's Beer near the refrigerator, where, apparently one could place the returnable bottles back into their original container after they were chilled and consumed.

There were two captains' chairs at the table, stained yellow and obviously matching each other but not the table. A third smaller wooden chair with a black seat seemed out of place. Its owner seemed uneasy, perhaps thinking he might have tidied up a bit before having me over for the first time.

A brief tour showed a path through what was apparently the living room area. Heaps of *Antique Week* magazines were stacked precariously in the southwestern corner of the room next to a stereo and a couple of crates of albums.

Rows of wooden bookshelves were built into all the back rooms of the house. He proudly talked about how the wall space between the six and seven foot marks of the ceiling was often 'wasted space' in most houses. Here, it was used to shelve books. There was the caving section, the nature section, the art bookcase. The bathroom was the *National Geographic* section. One shelf, in answer to domesticity, supported a few bath towels. We passed by the bedroom with its twin bed, itself below more shelves of books. The back room was an office area, with a central kiosk of office supplies, a small wooden table next to a tacked up calendar in the corner, and a typewriter where he punched out letters doing genealogy and local history research and letters to me.

The hallway had a bunch of clothes, coats and uniforms hanging from a self-designed rack in front of the washer and dryer. There was a pungent odor of moth crystals, which was sometimes on his clothes. That, he explained, was to protect his books from being devoured by moths, book bugs and other nearly invisible insects whose sole purpose in life was to consume his collection.

It was obvious, I thought, as I wondered what color the kitchen floor really was, that this place was merely a shell, a storage facility for his collection and a place where he came to sleep between forays to work, to do research and to take care of his grandmother's place in Mamont.

It was to that place, where he was firmly entrenched, that I would have to move when we were married. Neither of us wanted a big ceremony, and had basically decided to elope. We had initially planned the big "event" for the summer of 1994, but my moving in required that Tom have some type of addition built to his home or a storage shed built so I could move in. I feared the whole building would collapse into itself no matter what was done.

I had my own book collection, which was much smaller, my own record collection, my own furniture, a rolltop desk, a waterbed with two drawer sets below the frame, a personal computer with a five and a quarter inch floppy drive that basically served as a word processor, and my sports gear: a mountain bike, an all-terrain vehicle, basketballs, softball glove and bats, caving gear, and my writing files. Whereas he was content to store his files in used beer can flats, my stuff was very organized, each topic to its own manila folder, labeled and stored in alphabetical order. We each claimed to know where everything was with our own systems. Then there was my wardrobe. My sister Jackie and I spent a good deal of time shopping, enjoying keeping up with the latest styles and bargain-hunting. I had accumulated quite a collection of clothes.

Our marriage might have been hastened by several years had we not each had such collections, and no substantial means of building a new home.

While the quarry protest consumed much of our lives for several years, life outside of caving did have its own challenges. The summer before, after many personnel changes and cutbacks, I was asked by the owners of *The Latrobe Bulletin* to fire our editorial writer. Rich Kozar had capably replaced the retired Vince Quartrini covering county politics and had easily moved into the role of editorial writer. However, Rich had inadvertently been caught in the middle of these cutbacks and changes. I felt he was doing a good job, a very difficult job, and replacing him with any of the remaining staff members was out of the question. In a nutshell, I refused. So they fired us both.

I took a series of temporary jobs, some fairly long-term, as Tom and I had planned, in the summer of 1994, to attend the NSS Convention in Texas as part of a three-week trip to the American southwest. I feared I couldn't get three weeks of vacation at a new writing job, but when an opportunity came to write for *The Indiana Gazette* in February 1994, I talked a three-week unpaid leave into my new position as family page editor. The *Gazette* had twice the circulation of The *Bulletin*, so in the end I hadn't fared too badly.

Unfortunately, the job had no medical benefits, and not working for nearly a month was a hardship. In the end, it turned out that our planned honeymoon to the southwest was just another vacation, as Tom, much to my ire, had not yet had the storage shed constructed. There was nowhere for me to go.

By fall, however, we had contracted with a local home center to have the shed built on-site, so we set Friday, November 4, as our wedding day. It was just he and I, the justice of the peace and one of his staff members as a witness. My boss willingly gave me the day off and the morning was spent moving the stuff I could fit into my Sunbird and hauling it to Washington Township. My mother later said she knew something was up when both the dog and his dishes were gone.

We interrupted the move for our appointment with the magistrate in Indiana, and returned to the mess in the living room. The *Antique Weeks* had weeks before been boxed, categorized, labeled and moved to the shed—my doing, of course. Other dust-covered things began to be rearranged and more of a semblance of order reigned. The kitchen floor, I discovered, was a block-patterned white and gold linoleum.

The moving was interrupted on Saturday, November 5, by a meeting at Saint James, the former church where the Loyalhanna Grotto held its meetings. We were planning our strategy. The hearing on the quarry protest was fast approaching.

Paul Damon, Sr., had arranged for Janet Thorne, a prominent local caver who was involved on a national level with the NSS Foundation, to attend. Janet had been an advocate for the protection of Tytoona Cave in Blair County, Pa., and had worked with the Western Pennsylvania Conservancy in Pittsburgh to help secure its protection. She could, Paul assured us, provide us with valuable insights and advice on how to handle the various issues we were facing.

The somber crowd of cavers only broke a smile to congratulate Tom and I on our nuptials, then set to work discussing all of the issues we faced. There were many sides to each topic. Old issues were hashed and rehashed. New issues were constructed. Various strategic approaches were argued. The meeting wore on.

I broached the subject of negotiating with the Smiths. We didn't have much to offer, but we could, I suggested, see what their thoughts would be on dropping the protest if they agreed to leave the caves out of the mining permit.

Janet, who had been taking in all the issues regarding the watershed, the species of concern and the caves, suddenly interrupted my proposition.

"Look at what you've done so far," she said, summarizing the morning's discussion. "If I can offer you one piece of advice, one thing that you take to heart, then I must say this to you—'don't ever, ever compromise'."

We had only been settling into "our place" for a few weeks. I now had a square at the kitchen table big enough to place a cereal bowl without stacking it onto a pile of papers. Depending on what was for dinner, there might even have been room for my own mail. I was still getting used to where "my" things were—the cabinet full of photo albums in the former bedroom, my file cabinets in the living room area, which I had completely overtaken, my reams of documents and folders on the quarry protest.

Since all of the protest stuff was now consolidated into pretty much one site—the Metzgar abode, Chuck Hempel arranged for our weekend work session to be held at our place. The strategizing had been done, we had sorted out the issues as best as we could, and he had been busy studying the copy of the permit application we'd provided him, preparing his own versions of their topographic maps,

One of the displays that was prepared for the hearing.

with cave stuff, hydrology stuff, and geology stuff added on. We weren't sure what to expect, but he told us to have some assistants ready. By then Tom had gotten a computer, an Apple IIci, with laser printer. I had arranged its new configuration on a slab of wood between two filing cabinets, figuring he would get more storage and "filing" space than with a computer desk. The cabinets were empty, but the computer was ready.

Alex Boughamer, Lee Blazek and Bill Wolford were solicited to help us. Bill was Tom's age and had studied and worked in both geology and history and knew the ridge well. Alex and Lee were up and coming young cavers who both would go on to study geology, Alex at Indiana University of Pennsylvania and the University of Idaho and Lee at the Colorado School of Mines. Lee had done some dye-tracing work in some of the caves as a high school project. With all the scientific knowledge in the room, I felt I would best be put to use as the gopher, the low woman on the totem pole

Chuck asked many questions of us. While Bill and Tom, Lee and Alex pored over maps, Chuck turned to me every time a bit of documentation was needed. "Do we have any pictures of your claim of a major wet-weather resurgence in Trout Run?" "Where did Tasman make that statement?" "Are there any historic or archaeologic sites on the ridge?"

63

I would disappear into one of the back rooms while they continued to pore over the stacks of paper and piles of maps on the kitchen table and emerge later with the documentation Chuck was asking for. It became a sort of game—he and the guys would come up with some other way to put a crimp into their plans, even a minor stumbling block, and I would rummage around and come up with supporting evidence. We had to prepare, Chuck said, as if we were going to court, because someday we just might end up there. The DER, at its hearing, was going to require more than just a statement that the caves were beautiful, that they had streams in them, or that there were bats flying around on the ridge. They wanted cold, hard facts.

At some point during the day, as Tom jotted down a bulleted list of items to target, we remembered to eat and ordered a few pizzas. Chuck finally retired to a friend's house in Pittsburgh for the night, while we continued to work out the finer points of our strategy. By the next day we had our list.

From this emerged a 28-page document entitled "Report on Deficiencies in the Chestnut Ridge Quarry Application of Tasman Resources, Limited, Derry and Fairfield Townships, Westmoreland County, Pennsylvania."

Chuck Hempel submitted it on behalf of the Loyalhanna Grotto at the December 20, 1994 hearing before the DEP.

Hempel, having prepared many a mining permit application, and gone through the review process, knew we needed to be very specific in pointing out deficiencies. We had a hundred and eight objections referring to various modules of the permit application, citing chapter and verse.

Chuck Hempel's strategy was very similar to my original strategy during Clive Cutler's very first presentation before the Derry Township supervisors—to dispute every fact and figure they presented.

Chapter 11

The parking lot filled quickly. We had arrived early to prepare our displays in the Derry Junior High School Audion. The audion was a small auditorium, with a small stage up front. The DER had a sign-in outside the audion, and a few long tables set up in front of the stage. We busied ourselves tacking up cave maps and displays on the side walls of the audion. On the stage we placed our carefully prepared display boards—one on the historic sites that they had neglected to mention, one on water quality, and one on the wildlife that would be affected by the proposed mine. A caver friend, Dave Tanner, had even flown over the ridge and some other quarry sites, giving us aerial photos to present.

Chuck Hempel supervised the set-up, including some surprises we had been quietly working on. Chuck himself had shown up in a blue oxford shirt and brown jeans, with a pager hanging on his belt clip and a few pencils in his shirt pocket. That was it. He knew his stuff. While he sent Tom off in search of something for him to point to our displays with, I went out to the parking lot to greet cavers, friends and neighbors who were starting to show up. The newspaper coverage had gotten a good bit of attention in Derry Township. But to encourage people to attend, my dad had created flyers and put them in the mailboxes of Hillside residents. Locals were also asked to call friends and neighbors, and we had friends working Blairsville residents as well, since it would be that town's water which would be affected.

Grotto members would not be allowed to speak on behalf of the caving community. Instead, like Blairsville Borough, we would be allotted a time slot, which, in our case, would be filled by Chuck Hempel.

D. Scott Roberts of the DER stood up from his table to introduce the hearing and state all the necessary preliminaries, as his colleagues listened attentively, seriously. Roberts outlined the opposition by the Blairsville Water Authority and by us, as well as the meetings and review sessions that were held. He introduced the permit review team, which, for Chuck Hempel, meant going against a caver and friend from the Pittsburgh area, D. Scott Jones. Jones was the senior hydrogeologist within DER, and one of the lead permit reviewers. Jones was a caver, but he maintained a sense of professionalism throughout the process, filing his reports in accordance with his interpretation of state mining regulations. There was a wildlife specialist, a blasting expert, a mining engineer, and the district mining manager among the panel of nine experts.

Robert Garbart, wearing a dark suit, stood up with a sheaf of papers and made his way to the front, standing between the two tables of DER reviewers in front of the stage.

"I don't have anything to hide behind," he joked as he went into a history of his company and its qualifications to engineer the permit application. He noted in his presentation that a typical coal surface mining permit takes between four and six months of work.

This permit, its scope and involvement, took two and a half to three years to submit. He ticked off the list of experts his firm had commissioned to study all of the issues cavers had brought to the forefront: geology and hydrology, wildlife management and blasting, and went over a map of the proposed site on an overhead projector.

Next up was Clive Cutler, the president of Tasman Resources. A mining engineer for more than two decades, Cutler dryly began citing statistics on tonnage, truckloads, hours of operation and employment. He explained how one of the main issues to the quarry was its access road, which they had originally wanted to put through my grandfather's property, right past the Blairsville Reservoir. So they spent some time looking for another way out, to the south, due to "concerns" about the watershed. Not to mention, I thought as I videotaped the proceedings, that they hadn't obtained permission from my grandmother and the estate of my grandfather, to go through our property.

Blairsville Borough's engineer went third, like the two men before him bringing a sheaf of papers and talking statistics—number of customers, gallons per day of water treated, and other similar facts and figures that had the audience squirming in their seats. I shut off the camera to save on the battery as he continued to read from his notes. With all the engineering talk I was having a hard time following the details.

Chuck Hempel during a visit to another operating quarry to gath-
er photographic evidence of fuel leaks and water pollution.

Finally, it was Chuck Hempel's turn. He walked to where the others had stood, between the two tables in front of the stage, and clasped his hands together calmly in front of him, slowly looking around, it seemed as if at each person attending.

"I was asked here tonight by the little guys in this thing," he said, "the Loyalhanna Grotto."

Explaining that cavers were people who like to recreate in caves, he spoke on a level that everyone understood. Cavers, he said, were from industry. They were farmers, businessmen, environmentalists, "people just like you see here tonight, all united by a common interest in the environment and caving. When we first learned of Clive Cutler's proposal, I shook my head. We couldn't believe anybody would be so dumb as to come into an area in which so many people depended on for their water and propose a limestone mine when all up and down the ridge, all the way from Fayette County to north of where we are now we have a ridge full of limestone that can be mined."

The room grew quiet as he continued. Hempel noted that the mining permit application was the first bit of tangible evidence that mining was going to take place. Once the application was filed, he said, the grotto had again asked him to look at the issue, as a karst hydrogeologist, or one who studies the groundwater and geology of caves. After looking at the permit, he said, we had come up with a list of a hundred and eight deficiencies. The other side, he said, had spent a million and a half dollars on the permit work.

He started with the woodrat specialist, which, Hempel said, was from his alma mater, West Virginia University. "After four days of studies on the woodrat, he tells us there is not a woodrat on the site. A lot of people are saying 'who cares about a damn rat?' But the woodrat is an important creature to our woodland environment." He turned to our display board, noting we had documented 34 named sites where woodrats had been observed during the past few decades of studies by cavers. Gesturing to the pictures, Hempel described the "cute little fuzzy fellow in the nest. This high-falutin' expert—he's a nice guy, but not from this area—tells us in four days he 'caught me some chipmunks.' We'd like to help him catch a few rats."

Moving on to the hydrologist, whom Hempel described as "a well-known man, a reasonable hydrologist," he said "there is only one problem with this report. It didn't use any science. It's an opinion. Everyone here has an opinion." He outlined his own history of visits

Jennifer Hempel standing by a stream of cloudy water just below a quarry near Route 31 in Somerset County.

to the area, which started as a 15-year-old caver, then turned to our display board on the hydrology, noting that half the springs in the permit area were simply ignored. Copperhead Cave, their expert had said, was merely damp, not wet, and contained no flowing water. "As one who has walked through the cave in knee-deep water, I think perhaps there were a few things missed in the hydrology report." Huge resurgences, Hempel said, are open flow conduits draining the caves and the ridge. Even perennial springs were not sampled.

He called up his "assistants, Tom, and Alex Boughamer, both wearing our black and gold "save the caves" t-shirts. Walking up the stairs and onto the stage, Tom handed Chuck the yardstick he had found which would serve as his pointer, while Alex began unfolding the map we had prepared at our house a few days earlier. He and Tom held it up for all to see, as Hempel, still below the stage, dramatically pointed to various parts we had highlighted in different colors. He was attacking their sediment pond plan, which would have four ponds for the four different parts of the mine that were to be open simultaneously. The plan stated that no water would be allowed to escape without going through the treatment ponds, where the dirt would settle out first.

"None of the other quarries on the ridge are having problems with water," Hempel boomed, quoting from the report and turning to wave the yardstick at the audience, which was still quiet, attentive. "So Mr. Garbart and Mr. Cutler are not anticipating any problems. Mr. Cutler assures us that mining the top of the ridge off won't affect the water. As a professional geologist let me summarize what it's going to do to the water. It's going to be ruined. It's going to be filled with sediment. The infiltration patterns are going to be changed. You're going to have runoff in storms in places that aren't controlled. In short, you're going to have muddy water. Mr. Cutler says to us that because all of these other mines have never degraded the downstream water supply, he doesn't believe he will."

Hempel paced toward the audience, in command, waving the yardstick, then strode around and up the stairs to join Tom and Alex on stage. He stopped behind one of our display boards.

"I sent some folks out to take a look at those mines and here's what we found." He pointed at the boards, then moved the board aside to reveal a jar full of sediment. "The sediment was a mere 1500 feet downstream of one of the good example quarries, backing up to a depth of three and a half feet behind an old stone dam. He

Tom Metzgar gathering a jar of sediment from a silted up stone dam just below the Whitney Quarry.

grabbed another jar, this one full of silt, sand and water, and held it aloft. "This is what the water is going to look like down there. These are pictures of turbidity below the very mines that are being referenced. So now if this happens, if this is the example that is being held up to us here, to be used in this permit, if this happens, I think you're in a heap of trouble."

He moved into the geology, noting that the quarry operator had hired a geologist to do a linear features map. These kinds of maps trace underground and surface drainage trends, and often are an indication of subsurface drainage, such as occurs through cave passages. The consulting geologist, Hempel said, "came up with nine lines. I'm not sure where he came up with that from. I may ask him later tonight."

He waved the yardstick and on cue, Tom and Alex held up the grotto's fracture trace transparency overtop the topographic map we'd prepared of the quarry site. Hempel and his friends from WVU had used side-looking radar and high-altitude photography, as well as years of documentation and research from cavers. There were so many lines on the transparency that the topo map behind it was barely visible.

"We found out that there are joint-controlled caves in some of these features. We found that there are trends all over this property. There is more work that needs to be done here. In fact, if I was going to mine it I'd want to know everything there is to know about these fractures. Because along these fractures are caves or at least open joints. And Mr. Cutler, I don't think you want to mine air."

He continued attacking the geology and the many known features that were ignored, such as a major geologic fault on the east side of the ridge, which could affect the drainage and water quality. "It was ignored. That concerned me because it becomes readily apparent to me that whoever put this plan together, put this permit together, did not have complete data on the area and therefore the submittal and the plan perhaps is seriously flawed.

"Well, in a nutshell, what I'm trying to tell you is the mining company doesn't understand the hydrology, it doesn't understand the geology on this site. That's clear from their submittal. They're saying everything is just fine. In fact, they're telling us that it will not be an eyesore. This is not going to be an eyesore. It's going to be hidden by higher landmasses. It's going to be hidden by trees. Well for those of you who know the area they cut the trees down a few years ago up there. They timbered it and made quite a mess out of it. So scrap the trees keeping the dust down. And it's on one of the highest places in Westmoreland County. In fact, we have a book here, *Elevations in Pennsylvania,* which shows it to be higher than anything else here. So it's gonna stick out like the proverbial sore thumb."

He paced the stage, waving the yardstick.

"Well, that doesn't mean much here, except there's an element of trust here. If a man tells us that it's going to be hidden by higher mountains, and we go out there and it's the highest thing around, can I believe anything else?"

Hempel summarized the previous arguments on woodrats, hydrology and geology, just to remind everyone of what he had so eloquently stated. Then he continued.

"Well, we've got Dr. Michael's study that said it's gonna be no problem with these little woodrats," he said. "They have to be considered when you're talking about ruining the habitat of a threatened species. So I went to the Loyalhanna Grotto and to some of the researchers and scientists that work with the grotto and I said 'fellows could you go back to your journals and back to your photographs. I want to know every time that you saw a rat in a cave and every time you took a picture of one.' And if you look on some of the cave maps here, there are notes, rat nests. There's pictures on one of our boards here of a cute little fuzzy fellow sitting in a nest. Well we came up with 34 sites here, and I said before, documented sites, when this high-falutin expert, nice guy, but not from this area, comes in and tells us, in four days I caught me some chipmunks. Well, we'd like to help him catch a few rats, if that's what he wants. Thirty-four separate sites here, some in the permit, some out. If we had been allowed on the permit, I believe we could have found twice this many, just by going up and looking. So if you can't trust the mammology report, you can't trust the hydrology report, what about the blasting report?

"We've got our blasting expert here. It's my turn to pick on him a little bit.

"I am a licensed blaster in the state of Pennsylvania. I hold the license necessary to blast at this mine. I looked at this proposal right here that said we're going to leave a barrier around Copperhead Cave so that we can preserve those bats. Good intent. One place in the permit says they're going to leave 50 feet around that cave so that they wouldn't encroach on it, another place it said 100. Yeah,

More photos from water-quality evidence gathering.

the right hand didn't know what the left hand was doing. Unfortunately, neither is sufficient to protect that cave."

Hempel noted that he happened be a consultant for "a rather large mine working with endangered species in West Virginia. And on that project we concluded that 200 feet should be the very minimum that should be left. And in fact they're trying to leave even more than that because the threat is not just from blasting, but the threat is when you have a hibernaculum that you encounter the cave while mining and open up another passage and change the temperature of the cave by allowing the wind to go through, therefore ruining the bat hibernaculum. Well, we have a map here of the cave that was done over the last few years that shows that there are side passages" that mining could intersect.

Hempel said cavers believe from studying the map and the linear features map that Copperhead Cave extends further, and he was recommending a 500-foot barrier around the cave.

Summing up his testimony during the half-hour presentation, Hempel said:

"We don't believe that the barrier is sufficient here. We don't believe the hydrology report that is submitted with the report here is on the money. And we believe that because you have a fault here and a lot of fractures in this area, that all the springs in this area that are contributing to the Blairsville reservoir will be affected. Mr. Parizek (the hydrology person hired by Tasman, the mine operator) said when you mine this and put all the rubble back, you're going to increase the recharge and that's going to help Trout Run and that's going to help the reservoir. There's only one problem. If you've ever had a plugged drain because somebody put a bunch of junk down the toilet, you know what's going to happen to the pores in the Burgoon Sandstone when you put a bunch of Mauch Chunk shale into it and a bunch of limestone debris. You're actually going to retard, not increase the infiltration into that lower sandstone which is down in here, so you're going to get more surface runoff. When you get more surface runoff in an area that's just been affected by dozers, you're going to get more sediment.

"There are big problems with this permit the way it's submitted now," Hempel said. "Lastly, we also noted when looking at this permit, that the mine operator said there's no historic sites on this property, there's nothing to warrant archaeological study. He did not even show some of the old quarries which they're required by law to show. An old sandstone quarry up in this area, there's a couple little old quarries in this area, just small ones. They weren't even on the map, so the maps are deficient."

He said the grotto had documented seven old homestead sites dating back to the 1800s on the ridge, as well as two burial grounds, none of which were submitted for study by the mine operator. He pointed out that even the scale of Tasman's submitted maps was incorrect.

"In conclusion," Hempel said, "everything that we're told about how good it's gonna be, you're not going to be able to see it, that the water's not going to be affected downstream because none of the other quarries did, none of the other quarries affected it, everything they've told us about the geology, everything they've told us about the bats and the rats, it's wrong. It's simply wrong. This is the worst case of smoke and mirrors I've encountered in the 20 years I've been doing permits. I don't think it's intentional. I know Mr. Garbart (the engineer). I don't think that's the way he works. But it needs to be fixed and addressed. I urge everybody to take a look at our boards, take a look at the maps. Everything I've just talked to you about is shown photographically here. If there is anyone here that would like documentation on anything I just said, then see one of these two gentlemen (Tom Metzgar or Alex Boughamer.)"

Applause erupted at the conclusion of his presentation, and a few people stood.

Then officials from DER opened up the floor for comments from the local residents.

One of the Burry family descendants verified that there was a burial site in the proposed mine area.

My father, Ron Opatka, had a slew of questions, including questions about dust control and prevailing winds, residual dust from truck traffic, noise pollution, garbage pollution and traffic control with quarry trucks. He pointed out that Hillside is a residential community and wondered when condemnation procedures would begin on residents' properties to accommodate a 50-foot wide road for the quarry.

My dad questioned quarry operator Clive Cutler's statement that the Derry Township supervisors said they would accept the road.

"We haven't been invited to any public meeting saying that the supervisors are going to accept this road," he said, reading from the township codebook on the state regulations regarding public meetings.

Resident Dick Carlson expressed concern about the road as well as noise and air pollution.

Ken McFarland, a resident of Hillside Road, said his front porch is only fifteen feet from the road, and said he was worried about his sons and other neighborhood children.

Carol Miller, a resident of Old Route 217, said an artesian well she had in her yard was affected by installation of a fuel tank. In comparison, she asked, what will happen to the public water supply? "We do not want mining above our homes."

Caver Alex Boughamer also spoke as chairman of the Indiana University of Pennsylvania Outing Club, noting the recreational opportunities for students in the area.

A neighbor of Dick Carlson's said she moved to Hillside for peace and quiet, not air pollution and truck traffic.

Nain Sturges, who lived below the dam, said he was an avid fisherman and wondered what would happen to the native brook trout in Trout Run if a mine were to go through. He said logging done by SMT Family Partnership affected the brook trout, and he was concerned mining would eliminate them all.

Martha Jones, who at the time lived along the railroad tracks near where the proposed haul road was to come, wondered about her wetlands, the wildlife, and the road.

Ron Carlson, who lives at the railroad crossing in Hillside, said he was concerned about extension of the roadway.

My father jumped in again, stating that there is supposed to be ten days' notice for a public hearing on the road issue. The township supervisors, he said "kind of sold us down the river. If this were in Fox Chapel (at the time Clive Cutler's home) I'm sure the supervisors or commissioners of Allegheny County would be raising holy hell. Since we're in basically a blue collar and retirement area, it seems like our township supervisors really don't give a hoot in hell because it affects us."

Attorney Randy McCreary, representing the Jones (Burry) family, wondered if the Fish and Boat Commission had been included on the plan.

DER officials noted that there can be as many as 22 different state and federal agencies involved in a permit review, and that the Fish and Boat Commission was involved. It was noted that Trout Run is a cold water fishery and that DER was aware there was a concern about the water.

John Ankney, a Hillside resident, wondered who would foot the bill for utility relocation when the road is widened, and another Hillside resident wondered how it would affect residents' wells.

Gene Taylor, of Millwood, and the Derry Township Municipal Authority's representative to the Latrobe Municipal Authority, recalled a situation from 25 years ago.

Youngstown Borough had built a reservoir on Baggaley Ridge, he said, and once a quarry opened up above the water supply the "water became milky. And Youngstown Water became a customer of the Latrobe Municipal Authority."

Patricia Evanko, president of Blairsville Borough Council, said the council had drawn up a resolution supporting the Blairsville Municipal Authority in its efforts to block the permit, "because of the possibility of losing the limited water supply, the possibility of losing the holding capacity of the reservoir."

Ed Smith, at the time manager for the Blairsville Water Authority and Blairsville Borough, read a letter from State Representative Tim Pesci, who was in opposition to the project.

A Hillside resident said "I personally do not want Mr. Cutler to receive a permit for the quarry until such time as it has been thoroughly evaluated by all those concerned members of the community as to whether or not we want a quarry up there."

Ed Smith noted Congressman John Murtha had asked to be kept abreast of all matters involving the quarry, and read a letter from State Representative Joseph Petrarca opposing the mine. Smith also noted that PennVEST, an agency which helps municipalities borrow funding for projects such as water tanks and new water lines, was concerned with the proposal.

"Every drop of water that is in that basin we need," Smith said, recalling the three previous droughts, as well as the $1.8 million PennVEST loan for a water treatment facility below the dam. He also noted that in emergency situations, the Blairsville Water Authority purchases water from High Ridge.

"We pay $11,000 a month for that pipe (a 5.5 mile new water main). We pay $68,000 a month for our filtration center. If something would happen to that water we'd be out of a job. There are 5,000 customers in town. If we have to tap into High Ridge, who's going to pay for that?

"I think this issue should be a dead deal," Smith said. "I think everyone in their right mind would not support a quarry in a watershed, a fine watershed. We don't have a large basin. We have a limited amount of this water and we need every drop."

Terry DeBiase, chairman of the Blairsville Municipal Authority, cited the Youngstown quarry as an example. He added, "if something happens with this quarry that we have to go to another water supply, High Ridge is an emergency supply but not a solution to the problem.

Another Blairsville resident wondered if DER had enough of a bond for the operation.

Dan Duralia, a member of a group called Residents Advocating Good Environment (RAGE) tied in the Smith Family of the quarry proposal to a proposal they had six years previous to turn property they owned near Blairsville into a garbage dump. He wondered how long the application would take, the DER response being it would not be a long time.

Vic Smith, Jr., speaking on behalf of his family, the owners of the property involved in the permit application, said "we have the same environmental concerns that you folks have. I do have confidence that if Mr. Cutler's permit isn't accurate or isn't complete, that with all the experts up there "I'm confident that whatever decision is made will be okay. I have a concern that Mr. (Ed) Smith comes up and says how fragile the water supply is in Blairsville. Then why aren't you looking somewhere else for water? Why are you continuing to inhibit the development of our property?"

[Note: Blairsville Manager Ed Smith is not related to the Victor Smith family.]

Patricia Kowatch, a director of Blairsville Municipal Authority, spoke as a consumer of Blairsville Water. She said the borough had spent considerable money to bring its new filtration plant online, and since that time, the water quality has improved. Turning to the table of DER officials, she said, "If your job is to see to the wise use of Pennsylvania resources and to the health and safety of the citizens of this state you will deny that permit application."

Tom's sister, Heather, an Indiana resident, said simply, "Let them eat cake."

Helen Rhoades, a Blairsville property owner, noted the scarring of the mountain she sees when she looks out her window toward the Torrance quarry hurts. "What are we going to do? If y'ouns drill or mess up the ecology, you can't put it back again, it just won't work."

Dick Hedrick of Blairsville noted that early mining companies in West Virginia frequently forfeited their bonds because it was less costly to post the bond and lose it than to mine in an environmentally sensitive way.

He wondered if the mining company would be required to put up a bond, or "if there is a problem, if there is a risk, if there is a question, once something happens, once something is done, can someone just pick up and walk away?"

Terry DiBiase of the Blairsville Water Authority noted there was a reason his town built a reservoir in Hillside area, "Long before there was DER, we had a good supply of water in the Conemaugh River, and we all know what mining did to it."

Carol Miller, the Hillside resident who spoke earlier, made one last fervent plea to protect the watershed, for the "ecology, the bat caves, the rats and people. We're at the bottom and we're all against it. That's why we showed up tonight."

Ron Evanko of Blairsville pointed out that the mining company was touting the jobs it would bring to the area, but wondered if anyone had considered the industrial jobs Blairsville would stand to lose if they didn't have a good water supply.

Then that was it. What was very heartening to us, as cavers, was the outpouring of support from residents who cared about our issues as well as their own lives. To see a housewife from Hillside stand up and make a fervent plea for bats and rats, as well as for people, meant that these people listened to us, that they agreed with us, that they wanted the same things we did.

The only question we had left was, "would DER consider our arguments, would they find our points as valid as the local residents did?"

Chapter 12

We left the public hearing feeling pretty good. All of those hours of preparation had paid off, and Chuck Hempel had fired holes into every aspect of the proposed permit. We felt that each shot was solid, and judging by the audience reaction every time Chuck made a point, even a lay audience understood and appreciated the issues.

I felt that no matter what happened, we had given it our best shot. We had gone into the permit hearing and the protest knowing we were David to the Tasman Goliath. While we had struck some pretty solid blows, the requirements for noncoal mining are much less stringent than for coal mining permits, especially with the state's decision to remove the "Unsuitable for Mining" designation for noncoal mining.

Our answer came a year later: "NO." The permit to mine away Chestnut Ridge was issued. While deep down, it was almost to be expected, the disappointment was felt by everyone we talked to. It had taken so little time, in our minds, that we wondered if all of our points had even been considered. And while we had gotten by on expert volunteer help, copying costs, and presentation material expenses, once the permit got to the appeal stage, we knew that a small group of cavers would never be able to raise money to carry the protest forward.

J. Scott Roberts, Chief of Permits and Technical Services for DEP, signed Noncoal Surface Mining Permit No. 65940401 on December 21, 1995 for the Tasman Resources, Ltd., Chestnut Ridge Quarry in Derry and Fairfield Townships. It was almost a year to the day from the permit hearing of December 20, 1994.

The permit was for 970 acres of which 113.3 surface acres and 189 underground acres were to be affected for mineral removal. Additional authority to conduct mining activities was granted for an area of 175.8 acres, and the permit noted that authority to conduct additional mining activities could be granted by written approval later on.

In spite of the concerns about the Blairsville Reservoir, the permit allowed discharge into unnamed tributaries to Snyders Run and to Snyders Run, unnamed tributaries to Trout Run and to Trout Run, and unnamed tributaries to McGee Run, and to unnamed tributaries to Hillside Run and to Hillside Run. It pretty much covered all the surface drainage streams for a vast area of Chestnut Ridge. Overall, the initial permit allowed for disturbance of a combined 400-plus acres of surface and subsurface. The mine was to be huge.

The mandated National Pollutant Discharge Elimination System Permit Conditions and Requirements included such terminology as "bypass," or the intentional diversion of waste streams from any portion of a treatment facility; "severe property damage," "maximum daily discharge limitation," and other disturbing terms. Sure, there were penalties for violations of the Clean Water Act. But our evidence collecting forays under the supervision of Chuck Hempel were visible reminders to us of how other quarries had polluted streams and caused major sedimentation. There were 26 special conditions attached to the permit:

"1. There shall be no blasting on this site until such time as a blast plan is approved for the site by the Greensburg District Office and the

An old house foundation, one of many cultural resources on the property.

appropriate blasters liability insurance coverage has been obtained on the Surface Mine License.

"2. Any cultural resources discovered on site during the course of conducting mining activities under this permit must be adequately protected and their discovery promptly reported by phone and in writing to the Greensburg District Mining office and to the Pennsylvania Historical and Museum Commission, P.O. Box 1026, Harrisburg, PA 17108.

"3. Sufficient topsoil and/or subsoil, if encountered, shall be segregated and conserved to facilitate revegetation of those areas designated or specified to be revegetated in the approved mine reclamation plan. No topsoil may be removed from site.

"4. All water sample analyses results required under Part A shall be submitted to the following within one week of completion of the analyses: District Mining Manager, RR#2, Box 603-C, Armbrust Professional Center, Greensburg, PA 15601-9802.

"5. In the event the effluent limitations set forth in Parts A-1 through A-3 are violated for any discharge from sedimentation and erosion control facilities and/or the mine drainage treatment facilities draining to the Trout Run, Hillside Run, Snyders Run and/or McGee Run Watersheds, the permittee shall cease all mining activities until it has demonstrated, and the Department has found in writing that the condition resulting in the violation has been abated and that steps have been taken to prevent it from reoccurring in the future.

"6. In the event the surface mining and reclamation activities conducted by the permittee degrade the water quality in Trout Run, Snyders Run, unnamed tributaries to McGee Run and/or Hillside Run so as to exceed the applicable numerical water quality criteria set forth in 25 Pa. Code 93.9, the permittee shall cease all mining activities until it has demonstrated, and the Department has found in writing, that the condition causing the degradation has been abated and that steps have been taken to prevent it from reoccurring in the future."

7. [skipped in the permit]

"8. This permit authorizes variances to construct stream crossings on Hillside Run and an unnamed tributary to Hillside Run, as described in Module 14.

"The Permittee shall comply with the approved design plans, in such fashion, so as to prevent adverse hydrologic impacts to the streams within these variance area.

"9. Filter fabric silt fences shall be installed on the downslope side of all sedimentation ponds. These silt fences must be installed prior to disturbing any earth and shall be left in place until such time as the Department determines there is a good vegetative cover on the side slopes and top of the pond. The silt fences must be checked on a bi-weekly basis for damages or excessive sediment buildup, and shall be maintained in good working order, as determined by the Department.

"10. 'Dumped rock' energy dissipators shall be constructed at the outfall of all sedimentation and treatment ponds so as to prevent erosion beyond the outlets. A properly engineered aggregate filter or filter fabric shall be placed on the soil prior to the placement of rock.

"11. No topsoil, subsoil, or spoil shall be placed downgradient of the outslope of any collection ditch.

"12. All areas of the erosion and sedimentation facilities must be vegetated and mulched or rock-lined, as required by the permit of field conditions, immediately after construction and prior to the cer-tification.

"13. A two-pit variance is approved for Areas 1 and 2. Any future pit variance requests should include a history of the mining opera-tions in Areas 1, 2 (and where applicable, Area 3), as well as the specific equipment to be used in those Areas.

"14. All chemical treatment systems must be approved by the Department prior to the construction and implementation.

"15. Prior to beginning mining activities in Area 3, the operator will submit a) a description of mining operations in Areas 1 and 2. b) an evaluation of the erosion and sedimentation controls in those Areas, including discussions of any deviations from the original plans, why the changes were needed, when the modifications were made and how well the modifications addressed the problems. c) a com-parison of the post-mining effluent quality from sediment and treat-ment facilities in Areas 1 and 2 [including a review of all relevant pond samples in spreadsheet and graphic form] and d) an evaluation of how the discharge quality will compare to effluent standards imposed on Area 3 outfalls. The narrative will be submitted to the Department 180 days prior to the request for mining in Area 3. If the operator is unable to demonstrate the sedimentation and erosion/treatment facilities proposed for Area 3 will meet the effluent standards, no min-ing will be authorized for Area 3.

"16. The sequence of mining (Areas 1, 2, 3, and 4) as shown on a) Exhibit 9, and Section 9.1, dated 6/95 under the Seal of Robert Garbart and received in the Greensburg District Office on June 30,

1995, may not be changed without written permission from the Department.

"17. Upon activation of Area 3, the operator will add sampling point #62 to its regular quarterly monitoring plan. The operator will also provide turbidity analyses for this point.

"18. In emergency situations, where the operator's best efforts still fail to meet the required effluent standards for sediment and/or treatment pond outfalls in Area 3, the operator may pump the effluent via closed conduit, to sediment and/or treatment facilities in Areas 1 and 2. During this period, the operator shall cease his mining activities in Area 3 and notify the Mine Conservation Inspector of the situation and the specific measures taken to address this problem.

"19. As mining progresses in Area 3, the operator will inspect each new highwall face for solution channels and other secondary porosity features. If significant solution channels/joints are found in the lower half of the highwall, the operator shall photograph the section, describe the feature of interest, and document joint spacing, density and orientation and the presence of any significant groundwater discharges. The operator will also contact the Mine Conservation Inspector and technical services section, Greensburg District Office, via telephone, with this information, within 24 hours of the operator's initial inspection.

"20. Upon completion of mining in Area 3, the operator and the Department will conduct an inspection of the final highwall (see special condition 17). If significant solution channels/joints are found in the lower half of that highwall, the operator will provide the Department with an updated sealing plan for those voids. The operator must fully implement this plan as approved by the Department before the final highwall is backfilled.

"21. The permittee is prohibited from discharging wastewater into the Shirey Run and/or Coal Pit Run watersheds.

"22. The permittee may not use more than 20,000 gallons/day from the Trout Run Watershed for the mining operation. The operator may supplement the surface water with groundwater and/or surface water reserves from outside of the Trout Run Watershed.

"23. No soils may be disturbed and/or removed from the portion of the soil borrow area located within the Trout Run watershed until an erosion and sedimentation control plan for this area is approved by the Department and the controls are installed and certified.

"24. The temporary access road must be regraded and reclaimed by the end of the next planting season after completion of the permanent access road.

"25. Topsoil and overburden spoil piles shall be vegetated to prevent erosion.

"26. Drill rigs must be equipped with MSHA-approved dust suppression systems."

The conditions had shown that we had made an impact, and that the department had found a way to integrate some aspects of our concerns into its special conditions. But Tasman would be responsible for reporting itself to the agency, sort of like a chocoholic being placed in charge of sampling at the candy factory. They had won. We had lost. There was no way around that.

But December of 1995 followed two interesting developments in the quarry protest, none of which we thought, at the time, would have an impact. But both developments, traveling the same path cavers did, had repercussions felt even today, positive repercussions.

After the hearing held in Derry Township, we had given it everything we had. There was no ammunition left over, nothing more cavers could think of to do. We felt that the permit would be granted, and it was. We had demonstrated, without a doubt in our minds, the negative affects on watersheds, on wildlife, and we had "hired" one of the best experts on every issue in Chuck Hempel. Spending about two thousand dollars to Tasman's reputed two million, we had squeezed every bloody drop of water we could out of the Loyalhanna Limestone, our budget, and every drop of knowledge we could out of our volunteers.

So in September of 1995, when the Hillside Community Association issued its first newsletter, we didn't hold out much hope. And two months later, when the Chestnut Ridge Conservancy morphed out of an organization originally called Save The Chestnut Ridge Association, we wondered how much of an affect the groups could have. It wasn't that we weren't sympathetic. Many of the people involved with both groups did not hear of the proposed quarry until they saw news coverage of the hearing held in Derry Township, until they had seen reports of the issues brought about by cavers.

Meeting at the Hillside United Methodist Church, the association began by selling "quarry buster" tshirts, white shirts with a red circle and a slash through the circle overprinted on top of the word "Quarry" in black letters. Below the "no quarry" symbol were the words "Whatever it takes!"

Aside from the t-shirts, which were selling for $10, the HCA held a bakesale at Derry's Railroad Days to raise money for their protest efforts. Residents of Hillside baked the goods to be sold. The HCA hired an attorney, Dwayne Ross of Latrobe, who began trying to set up a meeting with Clive Cutler, Derry Township solicitor Tom Himler, and the township supervisors. The HCA's main issue was the route of the proposed quarry haul road, which would go right through old Route 217 and past the majority of the houses in the community. Their issues were issues my father had brought up at the original meeting, issues which were very valid, issues which, once stated, lit a proverbial fire under the residents.

Tasman and the SMT Family Partnership wanted and needed to get the stone from their quarry on the Derry Township side. Route 217 paralleled the base of the ridge between Route 22 at Blairsville and Route 30 at Kingston. "New" 217, as the residents called it, provided a much quicker and more competitive route for hauling stone to job sites than Derry Ridge Road and Route 259 on the Fairfield Township side of the ridge. Forcing the quarry operation to use the eastern flank of Chestnut Ridge as an access route for its haul road was akin to forcing the quarry to shuttle loads off the ridge via helicopter—not really viable and a financial disaster waiting to happen.

The SMT Family Partnership had attempted to say it had an access route through property once owned by my grandfather, Albert Smith. At the time of the protest, the property was tied up in a complicated estate settlement. Aside from that, my family didn't want the haul road coming past our houses, and we had stirred up enough concern about Blairsville's water supply that there was no way the DEP was going to issue a permit to have eighty trucks a day driving right past the reservoir. While my grandfather had operated a small agricultural limestone quarry between Hillside and Blairsville, we all were certain he would oppose any mining atop his beloved Chestnut Ridge. I was so certain he would have been on our side that as I packed up my video camera to film the protest hearing, I also tucked away a picture of him exploring Bear Cave in my camera case. I felt in some small way his presence at the hearing would give us strength.

So, even though I wondered what the Hillside Community Association could do to stop the quarry haul road, given our own situation with the caves, I was certainly going to do everything in my power to help them. The same held true for the Chestnut Ridge Conservancy.

With a haul road past the Blairsville Reservoir highly unlikely, the quarry operators looked at two alternatives. One was to use the township road in Millwood Hollow, and the other was to find an alternate way out in Hillside. The problem with the Millwood Hollow Road was that it used a one-lane bridge over the railroad tracks to access Route 217 by a very steep ramp-like road at the used bookstore in Millwood. There were weight limit issues as well as safety issues identified with that route, and the cost of building a safe, two-lane bridge and acquiring the right of way to do it, made that option highly unlikely. But SMT and Tasman owned property nearly all the way down to the railroad tracks at Hillside just south of the "loop" which led to the Blairsville Reservoir and the Bear Cave parking lot. They even secured a right-of-way from Thomas Pierce to go through his property and out the railroad. Only one thing stood in their way—a small house very close to the railroad tracks that had recently been sold to that one thing—a fiery blond woman named Maggie Rosbrough.

Maggie and her husband Jerry had just purchased their home from Martha Jones, whose husband Bud had passed away. With a pond and a quarter mile long driveway and several acres to mow, Martha felt it would be too much to take care of herself, so she moved into a mobile home about a half-mile away on other property she owned adjacent to the old Jones family homestead, which had been converted into a rental property.

Maggie and Jerry barely had time to move their things in—the ink was hardly dry on their deed—when the quarry protest and the haul road issue moved to the front and center of their lives. But the die had been cast, their possessions moved, and for the indeterminate future the quarry, the haul road, and the HCA moved to the forefront of their lives.

The HCA's initial strategy was to show that there were alternate routes for the quarry—that Tasman and SMT did not have to bring their trucks through the community. Later, the battle became much more personal for Maggie Rosborough. And, like my voice leading the caving community, Maggie's voice became that of the Hillside Community Association, a voice that would not back down, a voice determined to win.

The HCA called for political action, and listed the names of state senators and representatives for the district, and printed sample letters, which could be sent to those legislators. One of the Derry Township supervisors, Richard Shaffer, had died while in office, and his wife, Susan Shaffer had been appointed to the three-member board to complete his term of office. Her name and address was listed, as well as the list of newspapers for residents to contact. The newest paper to hit the streets was *The Independent,* a weekly in Latrobe founded by Rich Kozar, the *Latrobe Bulletin* editorial writer whom I'd lost my job defending.

In addition to Susan Shaffer, serving on the Derry Township Board of Supervisors were Chairman Lon Sinemus and Supervisor Lou De-Mary. DeMary had come out publicly in opposition to the quarry, but the other two supervisors did not respond to any requests by the HCA regarding the quarry. The HCA had given the supervisors a petition containing the signatures of 254 association members and Hillside residents who were opposed to the quarry.

While we had both been working at the *Bulletin*, I'd told Rich Kozar my views on the quarry, but specifically instructed him to form his own opinions as editorial writer, even if they were in opposition to mine. So, some months later, it was heartening to see his words, published in his own newspaper, in an editorial entitled "We, the people."

Kozar noted that Hillside residents had "interrogated, chided and threatened" the township supervisors, "accusing them of accommodating Hillside quarry developer Clive Cutler at their expense. Mr. DeMary was spared the brunt of their wrath, because he alone on the board has said he's opposed to the quarry. But the exchange between electorate and elected was notable if only for this reason: the residents reminded those they put into office exactly who it is they serve. And in the process, those opposing the quarry may have finally gained a toehold in their battle to prevent Tasman Resources Ltd., a.k.a. Mr. Cutler, from hauling gravel through their neighborhood."

Dwayne Ross argued that the supervisors had the discretionary power to prevent Tasman from using TR889 as a haul road, noting that the supervisors could refuse to bond the road if they felt use of it would harm public safety or the road itself. Without a road bond, Tasman could not use the road. However, the firm only had to post a $12,500 bond under state mining formulas, a meager amount. Kozar wrote that supervisors could "continue to make life easier for the quarry developer, or they can begin protecting the lives and property of their electorate. Either way, they may well end up in a lawsuit. But as one Hillside resident eloquently pointed out to supervisors Monday, and we paraphrase, 'Would you rather be sued by a big quarry developer, or citizens of your own township?'"

In the meantime, the *Ligonier Echo* of November 29, 1995, carried an article announcing a November 30 meeting of the Save the Chestnut Ridge Association in the Community Room at Ligonier Town Hall. The group had succeeded in getting an article in the Sunday *Pittsburgh Post-Gazette. The Echo* reported that the P-G article opponents of the project included Dick Groat, the former Pittsburgh Pirates shortstop whose Champion Lakes Golf Club overlooks Chestnut Ridge, and David Shapira, chairman and CEO of Giant Eagle, who owns property along Chestnut Ridge. Mark Samios, vice president of Save our Chestnut Ridge, reported that the group had hired two attorneys, and engineer, an air quality consultant and an environmental investigator.

Both of these groups were able to successfully stir up firestorms of protest within only a few months of the permit's issuance. Would it be enough?

"He (Cutler) is not coming through Hillside," Maggie Rosborough vowed.

Hillsiders are hot about proposed quarry road

By Richard Kozar

Although residents in the Derry Township village of Hillside fear they may not be able to stop a proposed limestone quarry on the ridge above them, they're determined to bring to a screeching halt plans to allow 80 tri-axles a day to reach it through some of their front yards and a township road barely 18-feet wide.

Neighbors say TR891, which begins at Route 217 and intersects a busy railroad crossing, is way too narrow and underbuilt to support heavy traffic. Moreover, says Hillside resident Maggie Rosborough, "I'll bet there's a train every 15 to 20 minutes. Now where are those trucks going to go when the crossing's closed?"

At a meeting last Thursday to discuss the road plans, Rosborough rallied opposition among 30 fellow homeowners. Relative newcomers to the town and the quarry controversy, she and her husband, Jerry, moved to Hillside on April 28. A week later, survey stakes for the roadway, which would wind down the mountain from the quarry and link up with the

Rocky start: Wooden stake marks the path of a proposed quarry road near Maggie Rosborough's Hillside home

existing township road, greeted her when she pulled into her driveway one evening. The orange-flagged stakes were sunk 75 feet from the front door of the house and four scenic acres the couple had fallen in love with.

"When I first saw the house,

I could not believe our good luck...or so I thought," she recalls wistfully. To preserve their investment and peace of mind, Rosborough agreed, reluctantly, to lead the fight against the quarry access road.

"I'd like to see Hillside get

organized. I know you people realize the impact this quarry is going to have on our area," she said to the roomful of people gathered at Hillside United Methodist Church, which openly opposes the road and offered the

Continued on Page 8

Maggie Rosborough working the media. This article appeared in The Independent.

Chapter 13

While Loyalhanna Grotto's participation in the quarry protest had pretty much come to a halt, I continued going to meetings: meetings with the Hillside Community Association, meetings at Maggie Rosborough's kitchen table, and meetings of the Ligonier-based group to save the ridge.

Tom and I took the shortcut over the ridge from Derry, meeting up with the winding Route 259 and heading north. The most direct route would have been from Hillside. If the Smiths had not closed off access to their property to us, we could have opened the gate at the Bear Cave parking lot, driven past the reservoir, up the quarry road, and continued down over the other side, ending at Route 259 and Shirley Hollow.

There, on a quiet, wooded lot, Russ Davies lived in a home where famed environmentalist Rachel Carson once summered. We pulled up and tried to find a parking spot among the many vehicles already there. Russ invited us into a roomful of residents from the "other" side of the ridge, and we sat in on their meeting.

One of the few things the Ligonier group had strongly on its side was the fact that very few members had known about the quarry protest. Most of the news coverage focused on the Derry Township side, and somehow the fact that it would affect "their' side of the mountain had gotten lost in the shuffle. They made a strong argument before the DEP that because they were not notified of the affect to them, a separate hearing should be held.

Like Maggie Rosborough and the HCA, this group was wasting no time in getting up to speed on the issues. But they were asking many of the same issues the grotto and cavers had already brought before DEP. As they ticked off items on their informal agenda, I couldn't help but interrupt, saying this had been tried, or that. The people seated throughout Russ Davies' living room kept giving me strange looks, looks of surprise, every time I expounded on an issue.

"You are not starting from square one," I told them. "You need to pick up where we left off."

Finally, I pulled out the videotape I'd made of the hearing and Russ popped it into his VCR. The room grew quiet as Chuck Hempel's voice filled the room.

"Who is that man?" Someone asked. I explained who Chuck Hempel was.

"We need him," came the reply.

"I'll put you in touch," I said. They asked to borrow the videotape. I said yes.

The members of the Save the Chestnut Ridge Association also listened when I suggested they come up with an organizational name that might better befit what was becoming everyone's long-term goal—to protect and preserve the Chestnut Ridge. It was the beginnings of the Chestnut Ridge Conservancy, as well as the beginnings—at least in my mind—of what would become the Mid-Atlantic Karst Conservancy.

CRC's attorneys were James Rosenburg of the Pittsburgh law firm of Marcus and Shapira, and Howard J. Wein, an environmental attorney with Klett, Leiber, Rooney and Shorling of Pittsburgh. Wein is a former Department of Environmental Resources attorney who understands the system, Russ Davies told the *Tribune-Review.*

In addition to the best attorneys, CRC also retained experts concerning wildlife and water and air quality. Dr. Joseph C. Merrit, then director of the Carnegie Museum of Natural History's Powdermill Biological Station in Ligonier Township and author of *Guide to Mammals of Pennsylvania,* commented on threatened species, primarily the Allegheny woodrat.

William B. Allen, Jr., a former reptile curator for the Pittsburgh Zoo for three dozen years authored *Snakes in Pennsylvania*. He reported on the timber rattler, which is a species of concern.

Chuck Hempel reported on geological, surface and ground water conditions and the potential affect on watersheds.

Larry Simmons, a professional engineer with a specialty in air quality issues, reported on potential for "fugitive dust generation" by the mine.

Davies, then president of the CRC, noted that the four reports included in the position paper would probably end up costing the conservancy between $20,000 and $30,000. But it took only thirteen days for DEP to review the position paper.

Just two days before Christmas in 1995 the media got word of the issuance of the Chestnut Ridge Quarry permit.

"Yes, it has been approved," DEP Deputy Secretary for Mineral Resources Robert C. Dolence told Dwayne Pickels of the *Tribune-Review.* The headline stated "Quarry gets state permit; Opponents cry Scrooge."

Dolence added that "participation by the public and the cooperation of Tasman Resources during the extensive review period has been very helpful. But the bottom line is, Tasman has met all of the required criteria. I feel we've gone the additional step in reviewing the matter."

In a very short time, the CRC had grown to over 370 members and prepared the 200-plus-page position paper that it submitted to DEP just weeks before the permit was granted. "It's unreal," said CRC spokeswoman MaryK Samios upon hearing the news the permit was granted. "You could have knocked us off our chairs when we heard. Our lawyers were flabbergasted, too."

Tasman attorney Harvey Eger of Pittsburgh told the media that Clive Cutler "was delighted to get word the permit was issued. Mr. Cutler's comment was, 'the system works.'" Eger told T*he Independent* that the "mine would be in production and have stone for sale by the end of summer [1996]."

On a third front, the attack was not over. John Como reported in the December 29, 1995, *Indiana Gazette* that the Blairsville Water Authority had hired Jones, Day, Reavis and Pogue of Pittsburgh to handle its appeal of the mining permit.

Como quoted D. Scott Jones, a hydrogeologist in the DEP district mining office. as saying 100 acres of the western border of the mining project had been eliminated because of concerns about the impact on Copperhead Cave. "The company has revised the original permit application and reduced the scope of the project to 870 acres," Jones said. "The mining would occur in four phases with the first two phases away from the Trout Run Watershed. The company will be mining the limestone from five to 10 years before they approach the watershed, and will have an opportunity to demonstrate that it can meet strict standards in protecting the watershed before permits would be issued in the watershed."

"In terms of major environmental impacts, the permit for the operation of the limestone mine and quarry is sound," said Jones. "There was nothing in the documentation of the conservancy that

Billboard erected by the Chestnut Ridge Conservancy along Route 30 in Ligonier.

jumped out at us during our review of the report."

Derry Township Supervisor Lon Sinemus didn't give much hope that the supervisors would deny Tasman a road bond, as the Hillside group had asked.

"To me, it seems pretty much cut and dried. If a man meets all the rules and regulations of the state on building something, he should be able to build it. It is the same with a quarry as with a house. If you meet the regulations, you should be able to build the house."

"Now we've had a setback," Mark Samios of CRC said. "It's doubly difficult for me to take personally, because it comes as a midnight surprise."

Maggie Rosborough told The *Independent* that she "feels disillusioned with the whole system." But, she added, "The goal of HCA has been to stop the quarry from using our road as a haul road. I feel confident the fight is not over."

Appeals, on all fronts, would cost money, and require substantial fund raising. That was one of the factors in Loyalhanna Grotto's decision not to file an appeal. We'd done all we could with $2,000 and all volunteers. Howard Wein estimated in a March 26, 1996, *Latrobe*

Bulletin article that an appeal could cost upwards of $130,000.

Mark Samios told the newspaper CRC was "dead serious about this litigation. We will fight tooth and nail."

The CRC and its new president Josh Wetzel also unveiled a plan to purchase the 5,000 acre SMT property, if the Smith family was willing to sell.

While HCA continued raising money on a scale larger than the grotto's efforts, the CRC began fund raising on a major scale. A golf outing at Champion Lakes, and several art auctions, coupled with wine tasting events proved very successful at raising large sums of money to fuel the appeal machine. Local artists—even Tom's sister Heather, who works in stained glass—donated original artwork that sold for hundreds of dollars per item. There was no stopping these people.

It took less than a month for the CRC board to file an appeal of the permit, a process that took most of the beginning of 1996. The first part would be collecting depositions from a variety of individuals involved in the permit and review process. Following the information gathering was a hearing before the Environmental Hearing Board, a five-person board independent of DEP. Following that, if another appeal was desired, the losing party could appeal to Commonwealth Court.

Just days after the CRC gave notice of its appeal, Tasman told the *Tribune-Review* it still expected work to begin "within the next six weeks." Company attorney Harvey Eger even told the newspaper that "the appeals are not going to interfere with our plans to proceed. I expect things to start happening pretty soon."

Listed among the officials attending a meeting with DEP and CRC were Garbart Engineering, Tasman's engineering firm; Victor P. Smith, Jr., of SMT Family Partnership; Bradley E. Smith, SMT legal counsel; and Dan Slavek, Jr., of Derry Construction Co. It was the first inkling that Clive Cutler wasn't the only person behind Tasman, as we were soon to discover that Slavek, owner of the one of the major construction companies in the area, was actually one of the chief financial backers of the controversial quarry. His name and affiliation with the quarry would become more prominent in the coming months, especially in connection with Maggie Rosborough and the Hillside group. And I thought back to the Trout Unlimited meeting, and the man I got into the argument with, and the name Dan Slavek fit with the face, and now made perfect sense.

Maggie Rosborough and her husband Jerry, and Martha Jones of Hillside (who sold the house to the couple and who also owned additional property in the area, also filed suit, a personal lawsuit, on April 26, 1996. Their Westmoreland County lawsuit claimed that the lower part of Tasman's access road acquired from Conrail, encroached on land jointly owned by Jones and the Rosboroughs. State road width regulations, as well as township regulations, were also questioned, Rosborough noting in her suit that Tasman's survey stakes for the access road were less than 75 feet from her front door. The stakes, she said, appeared about a week after they purchased the home in April of 1995. Part of the issue was that the access road location was dependent upon the center line of the railroad, and whether or not Tasman surveyors actually used the correct centerline in determining where that was.

Three months later, in July of 1996, Judge Daniel J. Ackerman ruled in favor of Tasman, another blow for the quarry opponents. Ackerman ruled that a conflict between survey results "is one that cannot be resolved with the facts on record" and that the "true boundaries could not be established to a certainty." He said the dispute was actually one of the use of the property and not actual ownership, and that Tasman had an easement to use the road, no matter what its location.

But legal problems weren't over for Tasman, as owners of an adjacent property in Fairfield Township also filed suit to protect their property from damage they alleged would result from mining. The suit was filed by Daniel, David and Ralph Shapira and Edith Shapira Schmidhofer.

The costs, both personally and organizationally were adding up, into the hundreds of thousands of dollars. Blairsville Municipal Authority reported it had spent more than $100,000 in its efforts to stop the quarry. The only good thing the opponents of the quarry could endeavor to enjoy was the fact that for every lawsuit filed, even ones in which we lost, Tasman was spending at least that much money to defend itself. So while Blairsville was raising $100,000, and the CRC was raising $130,000, and the other landowners were paying for their personal suits, Tasman was paying to defend each and every lawsuit.

Chapter 14

"Chestnut Ridge mine top of line, exec says." That was the headline in the Monday, June 17, 1996, edition of the *Tribune-Review*. This was the newspaper that way back at the beginning of the quarry protest had editorialized against cavers for liking bats and rats. Remember the "rodentophile" editorial?

Clive Cutler's photo appeared next to the fawningly favorable article on the quarry-to-be, calling it "the most environmentally sensitive" in the region. Cutler had just returned from Sydney, Australia, to give depositions for the permit appeal to the state Environmental Hearing Board and in lawsuits filed against Tasman regarding environmental and boundary issues.

Cutler told writer Paul Peirce that he had been involved with mining operations throughout the world for a quarter century and he had never been through such an extensive review process. He called the conditions imposed on him the toughest set of conditions in existence and said he was determined to make the quarry "a showpiece."

He was awaiting DEP approval of the air quality plan before site preparation could begin. Cutler said he felt when the air quality permit was issued he could begin site preparation within a few weeks.

Cutler, in June of 1996, told the newspaper that he and his wife Susan were the only owners of Tasman, but admitted he was seeking other investors. This statement would turn out to be crucial in yet another aspect of the mining permit within a few months.

He estimated start-up costs for the quarry would take between $6 and $8 million, "with all equipment, crushing plant, road in place. Susan and I have realized all along that we'd probably need additional investors because of the nature of this project, and the type of project it is requires significant capital expenditures."

Cutler also told the newspaper that he went back to Australia in 1995 to work for a civil engineering firm which designs highways and buildings, and intended to reside in Australia when the Westmoreland

County mine opened. "It won't be a problem," he said.

By fall, the permit had not been issued. And just when it was look-ing badly for Maggie and Jerry Rosborough and Martha Jones, who had lost their lawsuit in July of 1996, Judge Daniel Ackerman vacated that ruling only three months later. He reopened the case of the road boundary and access dispute for new information, with hearings sched-uled for March of 1997.

"I'm ecstatic," Maggie Rosborough said. And so were we.

At the same time, the HCA drew the Derry Township supervisors into the legal fray, alleging that the mining company entered into an agreement with the township supervisors in relation to the right-of-way for the road. This, the HCA alleged, violated the township code because part of that agreement modified a township ordinance illegally.

Every day I anxiously scanned the local papers, *The Independent, The Blairsville Dispatch, The Tribune-Review, The Latrobe Bulletin* and *The Indiana Gazette*, where I had landed a job. Following all of the twists and turns was like watching a daytime television soap opera. And I received notice that I was once again being drawn into the fray. I was to be deposed for testimony before the Environmental Hearing Board.

Paul Supowicz, an attorney for the Chestnut Ridge Conservancy, called to prep me for the deposition. We went over questions the other side might ask, potential stumbling blocks, and other assorted issues. If I was going to be called as an expert witness in caving, just how much did I know? I was not a professional geologist, I was not a biolo-gist, nor was I a hydrogeologist. What I "was" was a journalist who knew how to pull facts together from other experts and make them into a viable argument. That's what I was good at.

I dressed carefully for the appointment. Dwayne Ross, the attor-ney representing the Hillside Community Association, had graciously allowed depositions to be taken in his law office in Latrobe. This was convenient for many of the witnesses and allowed both sides to access lots of witnesses quickly.

I waited downstairs and chatted with one of Dwayne's partners, Leonard Reeves, who owned property up on the ridge. Then it was my turn. I was called upstairs to a plush conference room with thick carpeting. There, the attorneys waited, Paul Supowitz, of Klett, Lieber, Rooney and Schorling, the good guy; Zelda Curtiss, Office of Chief Counsel for the Department of Environmental Resources, and Laura Schleich Irwin, attorney for Babst, Calland, Clements and Zomnir, representing Tasman Resources.

Paul Supowitz was a young attorney with dark, curly hair and glasses. Like Jim Rosenberg, who ended up representing Maggie Rosborough, Paul was energetic, lively, and was devoting countless hours to the case. Zelda Curtiss was an experienced attorney, short, with graying hair, very businesslike and with an authoritative air. Laura Irwin was also younger, equally energetic, and about to lead the deposition. A court reporter took the transcript, which ended up at 87 pages.

The first few minutes were spent familiarizing me with the process, asking my work history, and about my relationships with people who had testified at the quarry protest hearings. Then they went on to ask me about how I had learned about the quarry, and the information-gathering process for the various reports the grotto and Chuck Hempel had presented at previous hearings.

The first third of the deposition involved them questioning me about the historic homesteads and other historic sites I had visited on the ridge, many on trips with Bob Eppley, my uncle Cal Smith, and my grandfather Albert Smith. I gave detailed descriptions of how to get to some of the sites, the more sites, I figured, the better—the more things they would have to study, locate and report back on. More dollars to add to the tally the other side was expending.

After that was exhausted, after about 33 pages of notes (and these are stenographer's notes, so they're not all that large, page-wise) came the good stuff, the questions on caves.

Again, we went through extensive questioning on the caves of the permit area. Again, I gave very thorough answers, mostly in line with the information we presented at previous hearings.

(Until noted otherwise, the questioner is Laura Schleich Irwin)

Q: Let's move on and talk about caves.

A: Yes.

Q: There's been comments submitted by Loyalhanna Grotto, as well as CRC, regarding concerns about adequate protection for caves?

A: Correct.

Q: Which caves, in particular, do you consider to be caves that should be considered by the DEP, with regard to the permit?

A: Well, I believe that they were already considered and removed from the permit area following the December '94 hearing. I'm told that Mr. Cutler, after consulting with DEP, voluntarily removed that area from the permit, and all that information about Copperhead Cave was presented then.

As far as the caves of the Hillside quarry, I don't think they were ever a threat, as far as quarrying, but we also presented information on the drainage, because we weren't sure. We felt more hydrological work needed to be done to determine whether they did, indeed, drain into the reservoir.

There are a few small caves on the eastern side of the ridge that we presented, and there are some that I've never been to, that I've heard about on the top of the ridge, because I heard about them after I had been asked not to go on the Smith property.

I'm not even sure where they are. I know one—there are talus caves called the Bear Cave Fire Tower talus caves. They're in a boulder field somewhere near the Fire Tower. I've never visited them. Those were reported by Bill Wolford and my husband many years ago. Probably 15 to 20 years ago they visited the same ones.

There is the Domal High Waterfall Cave, which is on the eastern side near a tributary to—no, it's along the power line. There are several others along the eastern side of the ridge.

Evac Cave is on the eastern side of the ridge. It's on Tommasini, Reeves and Downey property. It has a substantial stream. It would be included in the same Loyalhanna limestone spur that would be in the northern area of the permit. These springs drain off here (indicating). Evac Cave is further down on the eastern side. There is a spring draining out there.

Coon Cave is on the very northern end, and it's the second longest cave in the county with slightly over a mile of passage. It's on state land. They all show substantial—substantial water and springs emanating out of that whole entire Loyalhanna limestone spur. That information was indeed, presented.

We don't know about the geology, at this point, to know whether quarrying here (indicating) is going to open up this whole spur and affect the drainage. It's a mile long, but, primarily, from what we have been able to determine, Loyalhanna limestone parallels the outcrop—the cave passages in Loyalhanna limestone parallel the outcrop, and we were never able to break into anything along there to determine the relation between Coon Cave, Evac Cave or the three springs. It's work that needs to be done. It would be a shame if it wasn't done and they did disrupt the water.

So Copperhead Cave—I believe we presented a lot of information there. We had Eberhard Werner of West Virginia University present the fracture trace study, which the DEP should have on file as far as the joints, fractures and things like that.

He used side-looking radar and a bunch of other things, and he's pretty well noted in his field, and he determined that. That information was presented at the December 1994 hearing.

I believe it showed that Copperhead Cave drained directly into Trout Run, the stream, which would definitely affect the Blairsville watershed. It's a direct line conduit.

Q: Getting back to the first cave you mentioned, Copperhead Cave, you indicated that that's been taken out of the permitted area?

A: Correct.

Q: Are there concerns that remain, even though—

A: Yes.

Q: With respect to Copperhead Cave, even though it's been taken out of the permitted area?

A: Yes.

Q: What are those concerns?

A: The concerns remain that when Walt Hamm mapped the Copperhead Cave 10 or 12 years ago—he's a Pittsburgh Grotto member and well-known. He's mapped most of the caves in the Hillside area in the eighties and nineties before the property was closed.

When he mapped the cave, he mapped, I think, 3900 some odd feet, primarily in one joint pattern going down dip.

After he had mapped the cave, Bill Wolford had done a dig, that would be east of the entrance where he discovered slightly over a hundred feet of passage heading up and bordering the permit area.

Given the fact that Eberhard Werner's fracture trace studies showed a major fracture on the Copperhead (spur) and given the fact that Trout Run is down here (indicating), who's to say that there is cave passage—who's to say there isn't cave passage with water coming down that is directly in the permit area?

It's a major drain. There is a waterfall in the entrance. There are springs up here (indicating). Who's to say the watershed would still not be affected. I believe, without having read their report and without really having been consulted as their final, you know, report, I believe that could be what they're talking about.

Q: I'm not sure who you're referring to?

A: The Chestnut Ridge Conservancy, as you refer to in that question, as the concerns remaining.

Q: Just so I'm clear, you've not read the CRC position paper? Is that the report you're referring to?

A; No, I've never seen it.

Q: You're not entirely clear what their concerns would be, since you haven't read that?

A: I'm guessing, but that's—

Q: Would it be fair to say that the concern about the caves would pertain—because you don't know what the connection is between them, it would pertain, regardless of whether they were on the permitted area, or off the permitted area?

A: Our concern is hydrologic. With Copperhead Cave and quarrying above the cave, it is the largest cave bat hibernaculum in Western Pennsylvania. There is one mine, I think in maybe Armstrong County that has more bats, but as far as caves which contain bats, up until the Game Commission and everybody else was prevented access, it was the largest cave bat hibernaculum.

As anybody who knows anything about hibernating bats, if you disturb the air temperature, anything, humidity, things like that, any disruption there, that would make the cave ideal for hibernating bats, and could include loss of habitat and possible destruction of the bats. So we're definitely concerned about that.

Q: Getting back to—I mean, would it be true that there are caves on the permitted areas? Are there caves on permitted area?

A: I've heard rumors of the talus caves up near the Fire Tower, which supposedly have Eastern Woodrats, but I've never been there, because my access to the property was closed off before I had a chance to visit them.

There are a couple on the fringe area of the eastern part of the permit. I would say there's—I'll mark it, generally, somewhere here (indicating), and I'll put a circle with "Domal" in it. There is a cave called Domal High Waterfall Cave on the eastern side here (indicating), with a spring emanating out of it, which is a pretty nice spring. It's on the east side of Fire Tower Knob.

There is also a cave near one of the tributaries of the headwaters of Snyder's Run. I'm not sure. It may be on Shapira property. It may not be. It's in the area near one of the headwaters of Snyder's Run that also contains a pretty prominent spring. There are springs coming out all along there and all along the western side, Bear Cave Fire Tower knob.

Q: Would it be fair to say that the one, where you're not sure whether it's on the Shapira property or not, would be generally near where "old homestead" is written on this map?

A: No, it's near one of the tributaries to Snyder's Run. Everything is so marked up over here, I hesitate to mark it.

Q: Do you believe it to be outside the permitted area?

A: I'm not sure. I was to it, I believe maybe once, maybe several years ago, and I'm not sure exactly where it would be.

Q: Are there any other caves on the permitted area that you're concerned about?

A: Other than those I've mentioned, no.

Q: So with regard to the other caves that—you went on for quite a while, about the different caves and the different locations, the eastern side, and some you've never been to. I think you said some on the Evac Reeves property?

A: Right. It's northeast of the permit area, of the northern bounds of the permit area.

Q: So all of the other ones you mentioned would be outside of the permitted area, as far as you know?

A: Yes. but it doesn't mean that there isn't a hydrologic link.

Q: That's what my next question was going to be: your concern is that there is a possible hydrologic link between those caves that are on the permitted area and those caves that are not on the permitted are?

A: Right. There is an incredible amount of water coming out of the Coon Cave spur, which contains Evac, and the three springs which I believe is in the permitted area, and a good bit of springs coming out along the base of the Loyalhanna, the whole way around the base of this knob (indicating), sure.

Q: What is your basis for your statement that there is a possible hydrologic link between these caves?

A: I've been there. I've walked around it. I've spent years going up there.

Q: What is the basis for your belief that they are all connected?

MR. SUPOWICZ: Objection to the form. You can answer.

A: They're all coming out of the Loyalhanna limestone.

Q: I'm not sure what you mean by "coming out of Loyalhanna iimestone"?

A: They're emanating from joints and cracks and fissures and tiny little crevices in the Loyalhanna limestone, which is the cave bearing rock that they want to quarry. Why wouldn't I be concerned?

Q: I'm trying to understand your understanding for them being connected?

A: The Loyalhanna limestone is quite a water carrier.

Q: So I'm clear, all these caves—I've never been in a cave. I'm just trying to understand what you know.

A: Sure.

Q: They all consist of Loyalhanna limestone?

A: Right.

Q: If this room were a cave, we would be surrounded by Loyalhanna limestone?

A: All the caves mentioned, except for the Bear Cave Fire Tower talus caves, which would be in some type of sandstone on top of the ridge, which you would have to examine to determine the geologic stratigraphy, but all the other ones, yes, are in the Loyalhanna limestone, which is the primary rock to be mined.

Q: I understand. You believe them to possibly be connected because they're made out of the same thing. They're all made out of Loyalhanna limestone?

A: They're very far apart, but it doesn't mean that the water doesn't travel in the whole limestone spurs up there, through crevices that are too small for humans to fit through or from crevices as yet undiscovered.

Q: Have you undertaken any type of study to determine whether or not they're connected?

A: We've mapped all the caves. That, in itself, is quite a task. We just finished with all the caves in Westmoreland County. We had done most of the work in the Hillside area prior to 1992 because the Hillside has been a famous, well-known caving area since the 1950s and started from there. Those are where the known caves were, and that's where we started.

Q: Other than mapping the known caves in Westmoreland County, have you undertaken any type of investigation to determine whether or not, in fact, they are connected?

A: Well, to try to forge a connection, you do what's called digging. You go along. You look for air holes. You look for crevices. You look for slumped areas. You look for joints. You look for all kinds of different things and see if it's a likely spot that you might want to dig to try to find a cave passage. We dug into many caves, but never successfully in these areas, but that doesn't mean that they're not there.

Q: I understand. Other than the digging that you just described, anything else?

A: We had done some volume measurements on the three springs, as far as the volume and quality of the water, and had some interns do other stream tracing things, which I believe were published, in Shirey Run and in Trout Run. There's probably nothing that you don't have already.

Q: With regard to the springs that you've mentioned, a couple of them you described as "pretty nice springs"?

A: Yes.

Q: I'm not sure what you meant by that.

A: As fas as volume and quality of the water. I wouldn't hesitate to drink from them.

Q: I'm not sure how you would determine that they have a good quality of water that would be okay for a human to drink. Would it be based on the color or—I'm not sure how you would come to that conclusion.

A: They're emanating out of the Loyalhanna limestone. I'm not sure if we had ever done pH or other samples of those. You would have to ask Bob Eppley.

Q: Did you ever do any studies of the volumes coming out of any of the springs?

A: Bob Eppley did the three springs that are in the northern part of the permit area. I was with him at the time. I don't have the data, and I don't recall whether or not it was submitted.

Q: I think you mentioned you were up there with Bob Eppley prior to 1992?

A: Correct.

Q: As far as you know, since the testing that he did that you described, do you know of any other testing on those springs for quality?

A: I've not done any.

Q: Do you know of any that's been done by CRC or Loyalhanna Grotto?

A: Loyalhanna Grotto has not done any. Whether the Conservancy has, I don't know.

Q: A couple of times you made mention to the fact that at one point you were told by the Smith family to not go on the property anymore?

A: Right.

Q: When did that occur?

A: I believe it was September of '91 or '92. I'm not sure.

Q: Since that time have you undertaken any effort to try to gain access to the property?

A: No. There's no need. Most of our studies were done, probably pre-1990. We had all the data we needed. There is no reason for me to be up there.

Q: When you say, "The data that we needed," are you talking about the investigation you guys did—

A: As far as the cave maps, and, you know, the spring data that Bob Eppley did of the three springs. There's no reason for me to go up there.

Q: Did you ever want to go up to try to check out additonal information on the historic sites?

A: I've been to them all many, many times and have had them photographed. There is no need.

Q: Even with regard to the Burry site?

A: There is no need, unless I had someone to go back with and try to show me. My grandfather died. He had been to it many, many years ago.

Q: Let's talk a little about the Allegheny wood rat.

A: Yes. (Note: This was the moment I had planned for. I knew she'd ask me how to identify one).

Q: You've been identified by a couple of people within CRC as someone who has information about the wood rat?

A: Sure.

Q: Have you ever sighted an Allegheny wood rat on the permitted area?

A: Yes. I sighted rats, or signs of rats, such as fresh droppings or nesting materials, on two sites on the current permitted area.

Q: Could you identify those for me?

A: Sure. There was approximately an area—and this is very, very approximate because it was many, many years ago. It would be on the—if there was a better map—I'm not going to indicate, but I'm going to say it would be near—on the southern side of the Copperhead Cave spur near the westernmost boundary line of the current permitted area.

There were some small outcroppings of Loyalhanna limestone, some within the current permitted area and some extending beyond to the west of the permitted area, and I did sight fresh nesting materials and rat droppings right near this boundary line. The other also was a rat near the Domal High Waterfall Cave and some limestone outcrop on the eastern side of the Fire Tower spur.

Q: For the first one we talked about, could you generally identify that?

A: Do you see where the Loyalhanna limestone exposure is, where

Trout Run—marked on the topo the whole way up on the southern side of the Copperhead Cave spur, if you go and walk that (indicating)—

Q: You've drawn some lines and indicated 'rats"?

A: I've outlined the Loyalhanna limestone outcrop, as it's delineated on this map, Exhibit 8, and if you walk up and down there, the Loyalhanna outcrop is not continuous, but periodically you'll find different sizes and lengths and widths and exposures of it, pretty much the whole way up that side.

I witnessed, personally, rats in the abandoned quarry down in the northern edge of Snake Hill. I've witnessed rat nesting materials and rats in Spider Cave quarry, Byerguson quarry, and many numerous sites in the dry streambed and Trout Run from where it sinks into the ground below Hillside Run Cave to where it merges below Spider Cave quarry. I've witnessed wood rats and nesting material—like I said, nesting material and fresh wood rat signs somewhere along the southern side of the Copperhead Cave spur in walking this Loyalhanna outcrop looking for caves. I did witness a rat in the Domal High Waterfall area, as well.

Q: One thing for the record, Ms. Metzgar referenced this map as Exhibit 8, which is the number that's printed on it. For purposes of our deposition, it's Exhibit 1, so we're clear.

A: Okay.

Q: Do you believe that the rat you saw near the Domal High area— or however you referenced it—let's call it Domal for short—and near the outcrop on the—what side is this?

MS. CURTISS: West.

Q: West side. Do you believe both of those sightings to have been within the permitted area?

A: Like I said, you would have to precisely locate the Domal High Waterfall Cave, which I can't really do with all the markings on this map. There are wood rat signs the whole way up the outcrop on the southern side of the Copperhead Cave spur and all along Trout Run. I personally examined most of them.

Q: Do you believe them to have been on the permitted area, though?

A: Well, I don't recall, offhand, which part of the outcrop I've seen them on, but we had them located on the display board and on the copy that was submitted as evidence at the request of J. Scott Roberts following the December '94 hearing. So they're located on that.

Q: Do you recall when it was that you saw them, these two locations?

A: Well, from 1985, until, probably, 1991, when most of our work was complete. We were up there nearly every Sunday and, possibly, most Saturdays on the weekend. That's a seven-year time span. It's somewhere during that time span of our investigation of Chestnut Ridge.

Q: Do you recall, approximately, how many wood rats you saw?

A: Well, I've seen—

Q: Let me make that a little clearer before you answer. Within these two locations, the outcrop area and the Domal area?

A: I said in the outcrop area I saw nesting materials and droppings, which were fairly fresh at the time. I don't recall exactly when. In the outcrop area. The Domal High area, I don't recall when I was last there.

Q: Would you be able to distinguish between nestings and droppings of an Allegheny wood rat versus some other species of rat?

A: Yes. They're mostly—they're a woodland mammal, and they inhabit mostly caves and crevices. If you're going to Loyalhanna limestone outcrop checking for caves, it's a logical place to find them. They're little pellet-like things. There are publications, such as Joe Merritt's *Mammals of Pennsylvania,* that you can look to reference if you have questions.

Q: So would it be fair to say that you're certain that the evidence you saw on the outcrop side was from an Allegheny wood rat—

A: Yes.

Q: —As opposed to another species?

A: Absolutely.

Q: Based on your other sightings that you've indicated on other parts of the area that's adjacent to the permit area, could you describe for me an Allegheny wood rat?

A: I knew you would ask that. I'll tell you what. When we're not sure, we just wear a little T-shirt. I came prepared for this. [Note: At this point I removed my blouse to reveal I was wearing one of Rich Rosevear's woodrat t-shirts—not the Rat's Ass MAKC tshirts which came later, but just his pen and ink drawing of the rat]. They're not really rat-like. They're more bunny-like, and they're tan markings here with some white on the belly and a very long tail that's sometimes almost as long as the body. They can vary in size.

There are some that visit the Wolf Rocks, which is in the state forest in Ligonier Township, and they're quite, quite plump, because they get all these morsels from the tourists that go to the lookout.

A friend from the Grotto in Allentown, PA, did this (indicating). The nesting materials often look like this (indicating). They like to pile up big things like this with some straw and grass, and they often have nuts and berries and fruit and bottle caps, and we found a pair of eye glasses in one once. We found flagging tape that property owners often use to mark their property lines. They like to collect all kinds of little things.

They do not really look like a rat. Often, maybe eight inches, the average adult. I've seen the babies, too, and they like to cling to the mothers.

Q: When you were describing your T-shirt, it appears that there is a nest with a wood rat coming out of it and the nest looks like a big clump of —

A: It's the front on view of the rat.

Q: Their nest would be above ground like that?

A; No, they're in little crevices in the caves and in the rock outcropping. They often carry dry ferns and wild mushrooms and grass. You find poke berries, and lots of things like that, in their nest. In the fall, especially after the poke berries come out, they like to lay all the stuff, and it dries and it smells good. You walk along the rock ledge and you'll find all this drying stuff and it's pretty neat.

Q: What color did you say they are? Brown?

A: They can vary. The bellies are slightly white. They're often a light tan color, mostly on the sides and the tail. It can vary, depending on the time of year, what color they are.

Q: Have you ever participated in any investigations or studies of the wood rat?

A: Yes. My husband and I and other members of the Grotto documented 122 wood rat sites in Westmoreland County over the past six years.

Q: Have any of those documented sightings been on the portion of Chestnut Ridge that includes the permitted area and adjacent areas?

A: Like I say, on the Smith property, all of that was delineated on that large map that we turned into DEP. It was numbered. There were numbers placed on the maps, and then there was a key on another sheet of paper with the numbers corresponding to the site to determine what it was.

Q: So any sightings that you saw—

A: Right.

Q: —In the area of the permit would be on the information submitted to DEP?

A: Right. It's all prehearing, and it hasn't changed, because we haven't been there following the property's closure. All the information that we have should remain as stands to this day.

Q: Has any of that information, with regard to your investigation for the sightings, been published anywhere?

A: Yes.

Q: Where would that be?

A: We've published numerous things in our quarterly newsletter and in the book we completed.

Q: The quarterly newsletter would be the Loyalhanna Grotto's quarterly newsletter?

A: Right.

Q: The sightings, were they included in your book on caves?

A: Yes.

Q: The sightings that you mentioned down on the western side, did you mention—I don't want to misstate you—I think you might have said you saw some in the abandoned quarry?

A: Right.

Q: Could you tell me a little bit about those sightings?

A: Yes. There's an abandoned quarry on the northeast rim of what's locally known as Snake Hill. Snake Hill is on the west side of Trout Run.

Q: I think, actually, it's marked "Abandoned quarry." Is that what you're referring to?

A: Right. It's on the Smith property, and right over the edge is part of the Blairsville Borough watershed property where there's some nice prominent sandstone outcroppings down along there, and there are two very small caves in there that were documented primarily because they contain signs of wood rats.

One is called the Rubble Room. One was called Hillside Quarry Cave. They should have been noted in our conservation report that the DEP had.

In Hillside Quarry Cave, Bob Eppley and I dug into that, and there was a crevice that was yo wide (indicating), maybe eight inches wide by two feet high, and we dug out the fill in the bottom of it to widen it for humans to pass through, and it made an L turn to the left, and there were lots of woodrat pellets. Once we got around the corner and in, we saw wood rat nesting materials in that site, once we went around the corner and got into the cave.

Q: The caves that you are describing, talking about now, are those different from the abandoned quarry or are those caves within the quarry?

A: Those were within the quarry.

Q: Do you recall approximately how many wood rats—did you actually see any wood rats or just evidence of wood rats in those caves?

A: We saw the nesting materials and fresh poke berries and ferns that had been placed in the nest. Often, they go back in crevices when they hear noises like shovels and picks coming at them, and they hide. So after we dug it in, we saw the fresh signs and fresh droppings, which are indicated by being very moist and somewhat odiferous.

Q: Do you recall how many nests you saw?

A: One.

Q: Other than the sighting information that you've mentioned that you collected, have you done any other types of studies with regard to Allegheny wood rats?

A: No. That's it.

Q: Is there a specific time of the year that you're more likely to see a wood rat than another?

A: It depends. A lot of times, in late summer to early fall, they're more around their nest because they have babies and the babies can get to be quite big and sometimes they have multiple babies. They cling to the mother. The mother is often very visible because she wants to detract from you noticing the babies in the nest, so—but we caved all year round, and I would really have to check notes, as far as sightings, in trying to develop a pattern.

Q: Off the top of your head, you're not familiar or not aware of a particular time of year?

A: I can say that the rats are more visible after they had the babies, because the babies can't travel as far and they're carrying them around. You tend to see the actual rat more after that time, and they're primarily the mother rats trying to distract you from looking at the babies. That's when we've seen more of them.

Q: In its submission to the DEP on the deficiencies of the quarry application submitted by Loyalhanna Grotto, they make reference to 34 documented wood rat sites in and around the permit area that Loyalhanna Grotto has?

A: Right.

Q: Then the statement is made that if the Loyalhanna Grotto's researchers had had access to SMT's land, they would have documented at least 20 additional wood rat sites within the permit area.

A; Yes.

Q: Would you be able to identify for me those "at least additional 20 wood rat sites"?

A: My husband wrote that. You would have to ask him.

Q: Are you aware of any other wood rat sites within the permitted area, other than the two we talked about that you weren't sure of the exact location, but the Domal and one near the outcrop?

A: The only one I had heard rumor of was the Bear Cave Fire Tower talus caves, because we found that often the wood rats like to inhabit sandstone outcrops, and I never visited the site. My husband and Bill Wolford reported that years ago, and it was on a list of things to do, to go back and check, but then the property was closed, so it's never been done.

Q: Do you believe that the quarry, if it becomes operational, will negatively affect the Allegheny wood rat?

A: I don't know. It would depend on whether wood rats would be found to be occupying the limestone outcrop or the sandstone above the area to be quarried. If there are wood rats in there now and they're going to remove that, I assume they're not going to relocate them to a wood rat hotel in the meantime. I would say, yes, if there aren't, it wouldn't.

Q: If there were any on the permitted area, do you believe there are any steps that could be taken to prevent any adverse effect to the Allegheny wood rat?

A: Yes. Don't mine it.

Q: Other than not mining it, what steps could be taken?

A; Unless they capture them all and relocate them, I don't see how you could disrupt massive disruption of habitat with quarrying and big machines and destroying the rock above it and the ground.

Q: Is it possible that they could be relocated?

A: I don't know. You would have to ask the Game Commission people who study that.

Q: Is it your position that operation of the quarrying, other than affecting their nesting areas and their areas in which they live, do you believe the quarry operations will have an affect on the Allegheny wood rat?

A: I don't understand what you mean.

Q: Other than the possibility that the mining operations could affect their nesting areas, do you believe or think that the quarrying operations could, otherwise, affect the Allegheny wood rat?

A: Otherwise, how?

Q: In any other way that you can think of? That's what I'm asking.

A: Other than removal of their habitat, there is no other thing I can think of, unless it would be disruption of their water source, where they're getting their water. Pollution of their water?

Q: Are you aware of any studies of the effects of potential effects of quarrying operations on an Allegheny wood rat—or the Allegheny wood rat?

A: No. My realm has been to document sites, period. That's it.

Q: Earlier you made reference to—when I asked you about whether they could be relocated, you made reference to you would have to check with the Game Commission, or something like that?

A: Right.

Q: How does the Game Commission relate to the Allegheny wood rat?

A: The Game Commission census(es) wood rats and bats, primarily Cal Butchkoski. He is a wildlife technician. Up until 1992 cavers and Game Commission and anybody else was welcome. I believe they had census records.

Q: Would you consider the Allgeheny wood rat to be within the Game Commission's area of responsibility?

MR. SUPOWICZ: Objection to the form. You can answer.

A: I know it is.

Q: How do you know that?

A: We've had members assist with collecting the information and with their censusing of bats and the wood rats.

Q: Members of the Game Commission?

A: Members of the Grotto.

Q: Have assisted the Game Commission. is that what you're saying?

A: Sure.

Q: I would like to move on and talk about the bats for a little bit. You had mentioned that Coppehead Cave is the—I think you used the term "largest hibernaculum" or most-populated hibernaculum?

A: Cave hibernaculum in western Pennsylvania.

Q: What types of bats are in the caves of this area, the quarry permitted area?

A: That should be documented in the original Loyalhanna Grotto conservation report. It was based on Game Commission bat census data, which I believe, was made available to you as well. Primarily big brown bats, little brown bats, pipistrelles and occasionally a northern long-eared or keenii. I think they changed the terminology on what that's called now. It's pretty much all documented. You have the information.

Q: Is it your belief that all those different types of bats that you just described live in the caves in the area of the permit?

MR. SUPOWICZ: Objection to the form.

A: You would have to check the data presented.

Q: Right. I'm asking for your understanding or your knowledge.

A: I haven't looked at the information in several years, and I just don't recall, offhand, specifically, what is in what cave. It was based on information that some Game Commission employees provided me, and it was published in our newsletter, and it's in that conservation report.

Q: Have you personally ever undertaken any investigation in regards to bats in the area of the permit or vicinity?

A: No.

Q: Do you believe that the quarry, if it becomes operational, will negatively impact any of the bats living on the permitted area or around the permitted area?

A: I believe that there is a high likelihood that while quarrying may not specifically harm a bat, it could disrupt the bats' environment in Copperhead Cave by affecting humidity and relative temperature and amount of water which affects humidity which drains into Copperhead Cave.

In essence, I believe it would affect habitat, which could, in turn, either kill the bats if it happens while they're in hibernation and they experience a change or just disruption in their habitat and provide them no place to go.

I believe Mr. Cutler said they wouldn't be mining or blasting near the cave during the hibernation season, so as far as noise or other things disrupting it, I don't believe it's going to happen, if he keeps his word, but as far as them with this joint that extends to the east from the cave, sure it could.

Q: The basis for your belief that there is that possibility is what?

A: Is the fracture trace study done by Eberhard Werner, and my personal visits to the cave, and my personal observations of the water flowing through the cave and where it's coming from and the pattern and my personal observations of where it comes out in Trout Run.

Q: Are there any other locations that house bats or in which bats live that you're concerned about, other than Copperhead Cave?

A: No.

Q: When was the last time you were in Copperhead Cave?

A: Two months before the Smiths asked me not to go in there. It was in July of —I would have to check the year. It was either '91 or '92. We undertook the video, which we submitted to the DEP, which should be on file.

Q: When you say that Copperhead Cave is the largest bat hibernaculum in Western Pennsylvania—

A: Cave bat hibernaculum, because there is a mine bat hibernaculum that's larger.

Q: It's a cave bat hibernaculum. It was the largest one as of what date? Do you know? Is that current?

A: No. Because I don't believe anybody has done bat censusing since the property was closed. That was current, as of, I believe, 1992 Game Commission. You would have to check with the Game Commission.

Q: Earlier I think you made reference to—this could also be something I read. Did the DEP or the Game Commission or any other state agency put up gates or something, on this cave?

A: I've heard, from hunters who have permission to hunt on the property, that there are gates, but I've never personally observed them.

Q: Do you know why gates would have been put up there?

A: I don't know. I didn't put them there.

Q: Do you know why the Smiths have restricted access to their property?

A: You would have to talk to the Smiths.

Q: So far, we've talked about potential effects of the quarrying operation on the caves. Outside of quarrying operations, are there any other types of activities that can negatively impact caves? By "negatively impact" I would mean the water level that would affect the bats and things like that.

A: Not that I know of.

Q: Is there any other type of industrial activity that would affect them, or could affect them, rather?

MR. SUPOWICZ: Object as to form. It's very overbroad and calling for speculation, but you can answer.

Q: What I'm trying to establish, is the only thing that could possibly negatively impact Copperhead Cave a quarry? Could anything else that humans do to negatively affect—

A: Caves in general?

Q: Copperhead Cave. Let's talk about that one.

A: Sure. From that aspect, say, they were to undertake, even a mushroom mine or something. If they had quarried it out, certainly the fertilizers and things like that could eventually leach into the water. Certainly, putting a solid waste treatment facility in relation to the quarry might. A nuclear reactor. Anything. You're being so general, it's hard to pinpoint what—they could do solid waste disposal. Sure. There are tons of things, if you're going to make it so general.

Q: Could residential development in the general vicinity, say, down-hill side, could that negatively affect any of the caves on the permitted area?

MR. SUPOWICZ: I'm going to object. This is speculation. This is not an expert witness. I'm not going to instruct her not to answer the question.

MS. IRWIN: Right.

Q: I'm trying to understand if there is anything else that—

A: You mean the houses in Hillside that are there now could impact a cave?

Q: Right.

A: No. It's relatively impossible. It's slightly below 2500 feet in elevation. The elevation in the town of Hillside is—you're getting way down. They're 1200 feet. If they put a pipeline in and pump it up to the cave, what are they going to do?

MS. IRWIN: Can you mark that?

(whereupon Metzgar Exhibit No. 2 was marked for identification).

Q: If you can take a look at what's been marked Exhibit No. 2?

A: Um-hmmm.

Q: Could you identify for me what this is?

A: Sure. It was a statement which was attached to petitions that Loyalhanna Grotto presented to the DER office showing people who are upset with the proposed quarry.

Q: Is this your handwriting that's at the bottom of the page?

A: No, it is not. Well now—let's see.

MR. SUPOWICZ: Which handwriting are you talking about?

A: My handwriting says, "Return signed petitions to," and I have a stamp with my old address on it. Below that it says, "If you've already signed, get two more signatures." That's my handwriting. The other is not.

Q: Do you recall if, at one point the Loyalhanna Grotto had any plans to install any type of gate at the entrance of Copperhead Cave?

A: Not at Copperhead Cave.

Q: What cave do you recall?

A: Well, we had discussed something about Copperhead Cave, but there were never any plans. There was also discussion—we've never had plans to gate any of the caves, but we discussed the pros and cons of gating, just because it was an issue at the time. Also, a discussion about gating a new section with a lot of nice formations in Con Cave, but not the whole thing.

It never even approached the point where we contacted land owners with the proposal. It was brought up, at one point, by someone at a meeting. I don't remember who. We discussed it, and nothing ever happened.

Q: Earlier in this litigation we took the deposition of Mr. Hempel, who I think you referenced his name. He indicated that you handled the issues in the Loyalhanna Grotto with regard to lighting and noise. Is that accurate?

A: No. That was my husband.

Q: Did you provide Mr. Hempel with aerial photographs of the quarry permit area?

A: I had them in my possession. I did not take them. They were taken by Dave Tanner of Pittsburgh.

Q: Do you know when they were taken?

A: I don't recall.

Q: I think I may have asked you this, but just in case I didn't, with regard to the springs that you identified—

A: Yes.

Q: —did you undertake any studies or any investigation with regard to the volume of those springs or the flow rates?

A: Yes. Bob Eppley took volume measurements at the three springs.

Q: Other than what Mr. Eppley did, were you involved in any other investigation of that nature?

A: On the quarry property?

Q: Right.

A: No.

Q: How about outside the quarry property?

A: Yes. Loyalhanna Grotto had an intern by the name of Michael Guzo who did some water sampling along Trout Run below the Smith property and also in Shirey Run. He did sampling and pH assessments of the water.

Q: You believe that's reported in one of your newsletters?

A: Correct.

Q: Do you know what Mr. Eppley did with the results of the measures that he took?

A: No, I do not.

Q: Have you ever made any proposals to the Smiths about an agreement, or some type of arrangement that could be made to allow entry onto the Smith property?

A: Since it's been closed?

Q: Right. which I believe you indicated was '91 or '92?

A: No. I've never approached them.

Q: During his deposition, Mr. Hempel was asked whether or not he had ever asked the Smiths for permission to enter the property in order to take samples, and he responded that there was a proposal at one time made by Loyalhanna Grotto, Kim Metzgar, in particular, that we would accompany DEP and show them the items we are concerned about and that was turned down?

A: That wasn't our proposal. I believe that was after the hearing when J. Scott Roberts or Scott Jones was asking us about these sites, and I believe it was just a general thing: "if you need us to go up there and show you where anything is, we would be glad to do it."

They never got back to us and we never made an effort—it wasn't our duty to go and collect samples, but when we presented the map, we felt if there was a place they were unable to locate or needed help in locating we would be glad to do it if they could secure permission.

Q: By "they," you're referring to DEP?

A: Correct.

Q: After which meeting was this? The December 20, 1994 meeting?

A: In conversation following the public hearing in December of '94, yes.

Q: Other than information about the caves, the springs, the homesteads and the burial sites and the wood rat and the bats, is there any other general topic of information for which you provided input to the Loyalhanna report?

A: Photographs.

Q: Anything else?

A. Not that I recall.

That pretty much ended the deposition. I only hoped that the loads of testimony I had willingly given, collected from fun trips as a hobbyist, would cost them tons of money to analyze, study and respond to.

Chapter 15

Much as I wasn't afraid to stand up to the Smiths, or lead protests about the quarry, I didn't like to cross the line when it came to doing things I wasn't supposed to do. But we had never gathered all of the data we thought we could, and sometimes the thought of finding just one more woodrat site, or checking out one more cave lead would entice one of us cavers to try and sneak up onto the ridge thinking the Smiths wouldn't catch us.

One humid afternoon Tom and I and the dog started on the Blairsville Borough property, checking the sandstone outcrop on the western slope of Trout Run for signs of woodrats. The laurel got so thick we soon found ourselves soaked, on all fours, scooting along just like Nate. The low hum of bees up ahead made me halt, slowly back up, and wonder what in the world we were doing. "That's enough," I said to Tom. "I think we have enough data."

We knew enough locals, and people with ties to the Smiths that we were able to keep up on what was going on up there. Rumors of road-building, tree-cutting, big gaps seen from afar in what had been continual forest, were enough to drive us crazy with wonder. One Saturday after we'd done an Adopt-A-Highway, a group of cavers went up to Bear Cave to pick up litter and do some caving. Tom persuaded me to take my all-terrain vehicle down from Bear Cave past the Con Cave quarry so he could check out the rumored haul road work.

"It's only one-way, less than a mile, and who's going to be there at this time on a Saturday afternoon?"

Two people on my 200SX really made it less maneuverable, and we had just driven past the lower part of the quarry when we heard equipment, saw pickup trucks and signs of activity on the road below us.

Cursing at myself for being persuaded to trespass, I skidded to a halt as quietly as skidding allowed, put it in reverse and didn't care what kind of ride Tom experienced as I bumped over the rough road to safe territory.

The sight of all the workmen had worked up Tom's curiosity, and speculation about what the Smiths were up to was driving him crazy. And Tom being driven crazy naturally meant I was being driven crazy, so I reluctantly, very reluctantly, agreed to go on one more excursion.

"Friday night, they'll never be up there on a Friday night," he said. We waited till nightfall. I stopped the ATV at the end of the tram road and we listened for quite some time. Nothing but crickets and a slight breeze. Finally, not able to put it off any longer, I started the machine and headed up the quarry road. I had just turned off onto the road where we had seen the workmen, poised to go down the hill, Tom's arms around my waist, when out of the blackness a set of truck headlights came on, pointing right in our direction. The vehicle started forward. I couldn't tell who the person was behind the headlights, but I pictured it being one of my relatives. I imagined the local magistrate's office, my relatives grinning as they had me arrested, publicity, all that stuff. I froze for a moment.

Then Tom sprung into action, like a finely choreographed television show. He rolled off the back, into the bushes, and down the side of the hill in what seemed like one motion. I quickly put the ATV into reverse and once back on the quarry road, I had that four-wheeler going so fast that at one point the only body parts I remember touching the quad were my two hands on the handlebars. I sped down the tram road afraid to look back to see how close the truck was to me, sped through the Bear Cave parking lot and pulled in behind my parents' shed. I didn't think I had enough time to pull into the shed, so I sat behind it, breathing heavily, wondering if Tom would get caught, and if they'd figure out who I was.

That was it, I vowed. I didn't care what they were doing up on that ridge, there was no way I was ever going up there again unless I was permitted, legally, and the owners knew about it.

Thus, many months into our protest, I had arranged to take a day off work from The Indiana Gazette—unpaid—to spend a highly anticipated day on a court-ordered field visit to Chestnut Ridge. I had not been up on the ridge much since the property had been closed to us by the Smith family. But on that rainy, rainy, October day, there was nothing they could do to keep me off.

Tom and I met Chuck Hempel, caver Jen Dallatore, and a number of members and attorneys for the Chestnut Ridge Conservancy for the first site visit to the proposed quarry site. The purpose of the visit was to give the opposite side (the Chestnut Ridge Conservancy) a chance to visit and document some of the areas in dispute regarding the quarry.

We were to split up in several groups. It was decided after several long bouts of legal wrangling, that each group representing the CRC would be tailed by a group representing Garbart Engineering, the engineering firm for the quarry, and occasionally by an attorney from the other side. Tom had the opportunity to have Vic Smith, Jr., of the SMT Family Partnership accompany his group, as well as Dr. Joe Merritt of Powdermill Nature Reserve, the eminent mammalogist. Tom and Dr. Merritt were to look for woodrats. I'm sure my cousin Vic was hoping they wouldn't find any.

Chuck Hempel had wanted as many people assisting him as possible, and once we started, I understood his strategy: the more people we had out in the field, the more data we could gather. Additionally, the more data we gathered, the more data we could use against them. And the more data the opponents would have to study to fight our appeals and lawsuits.

Chuck assigned Jen and I to look for woodrats as well, on the northern side of the Copperhead Cave spur. We had all gathered at the meadow at the top of the ridge. As Jen and I walked along the main road toward our destination, I saw an interesting mix of rocks in the road and casually scooped up a handful of pebbles to look at them.

"Hey, hold on a minute." Our dark-haired tail from the engineering firm quickened his pace. "What are you doing?"

"What?" I looked at Jen in puzzlement.

"You can't do that."

"Do what?"

"I need to see what you have in your hand."

I looked down at the pebbles, which I had been about to discard.

"I just scooped these up from the road to look at them."

"Which part of the road?" he asked, pulling a bag out of his pack as if to collect a sample.

"I don't know, somewhere in the road. I was just looking at them. I didn't really want them." I tossed them back down, afraid to look at Jen, an idea germinating in my head. It continued to rain, and we began the long downhill walk, wending our way through a thicket of mountain laurel on our way to find the limestone outcrop. Greenbriers plucked at our raincoats and little rivulets of runoff welled up and began working their way down the Trout Run Valley. When I found a particularly miserable looking site, I couldn't resist, looked at Jen, and got down on my hands and knees, crawling under dripping laurel leaves and branches to where runoff water was flowing out from under a rock. I grabbed some sand in my hand, crawled back out, reached into my pack, pulled out a baggie and stuck the sand in. I looked at Jen; we looked at our brown-haired engineer, and waited for him to collect his sample. It was all we could do to contain ourselves. He didn't know our job was just to look for woodrats, and I wouldn't have known what to do with the "samples" I collected. But we oh so enjoyed having him crawl under the bushes.

We made our way along the limestone outcrop, checking for woodrats. We found none, and no fresh signs, then made our way to the Copperhead Cave entrance and saw the gate with no door that the Smiths had put on the entrance. Jen and I took pictures of our trip, but my roll of film didn't come out for some reason.

No woodrats in sight, we undertook our second task of the day, later meeting up with Chuck, Tom and many engineers and attorneys. We were to document wetlands areas that the grotto had brought up in its original protest material to DEP, wetlands sites which never seemed to have been addressed. But all that rain and all that talk of water was causing an uncomfortable feeling in my bladder, one of fullness, one of pressure. I looked around. Everyone else had been there three or four hours. I didn't know what they did, but there were no facilities. Finally, I could take it no more and headed for an out of the way dirt pile to hide behind.

"Hold it!"

I turned. Laura Schleich Irwin, counsel for Tasman, was waving her hand at me. "You can't go over there."

Howard Wein stood next to her and waved me back.

"I didn't think you all wanted to watch me water a tree," I said and kept going. "But if someone wants a sample..."

The rain continued and I thought of all of those nasty, nasty hikes Tom and I had taken while doing work on the *Caves of Westmoreland County* book and knew that this was a piece of cake in comparison. We were in our element, and that element was rain. Chuck and the attorneys vetoed me showing the other side Lost Hat Cave and some other caves we had discovered on the east side of

A fence lizard discovered during the site visit.

the Fire Tower spur due to the rain, and we headed down the mountain to the Con Cave Quarry.

Anyone who knows Tom knows his fondness for things reptilian, ugly, stinky and slimy. Just like a kid, whether it be a slimy salamander, a snake, or some other slithering creature. Once he determined what it was and whether or not it was safe to pick it up, he would quickly snatch it up, look at it, put it back down, and then try to find a water source to wash the salamander slime or the stink or the toad pee off his hands. As we stood at the base of the slope leading up to the Con Cave entrance I saw a small, dark critter on the ground. I kept looking at Tom hoping he'd see it, but when he didn't, cringing the whole time, I bent over and scooped it up in my hands.

"What is this?" I asked, quickly gathering a crowd. Tom made me hold it while he took a picture, and from the perspective of the attorneys on the opposing side you'd have thought I'd just found a crown jewel. Chuck Hempel acted that way, Tom acted that way, but oddly didn't spout off some Latin name for fence lizard. It took me a few moments to figure out that they weren't giving the other side any information whatsoever—they were going to make them work for every little bit of data. Before we left, I trotted up the slope to the Con Cave entrance, wanting to have my picture taken by the Smith's gate-with-no-door.

Once again, the shouts of attorneys warned me not to go inside. Yeah, right, I thought. No helmet, no light, like I was really going to squeeze in between the rebar. I thought of the warning labels on consumer products and began imagining what labels they'd put on cave entrances. I smiled for the photo, and then headed down to the truck.

We did a hike up Trout Run, looking at some of the water resurgences in the Loyalhanna Limestone in the streambed, then ended the day down at Maggie Rosborough's house, the rain finally letting up, as everyone looked at the projected right of way for the quarry.

Chapter 16

In the meantime, with a date before the State Environmental Hearing Board looming, in true soap-opera-like fashion, another Tasman Resources secret had been revealed. It was something that hearkened back to a puzzling scene in January of 1993—remember Tom's presentation (see Chapter 8) to the Forbes Trail Chapter of Trout Unlimited—and my angry outburst as a member of the audience kept trying to poke holes in our presentation. The man in the audience that day had been Dan Slavek, Jr., owner of Derry Construction Co,

In November of 1996, only two months before the state Environmental Hearing Board was to hear the case, the Chestnut Ridge Conservancy revealed that Clive and Susan Cutler were NOT the sole owners of Tasman Resourcess, and that two businessmen with construction business ties were actually the primary owners and investors of Tasman Resources. That explained Cutler's puzzling statement in the summer about running the quarry from Australia—he wouldn't be needed because Dan Slavek, Jr., of Derry Construction Co, and James Johnson, of Russell Standard Corp., were principals, partners and owners in the business.

The CRC said Johnson invested $200,000 in the quarry proposal, and Slavek more than $750,000. Cutler's total investment was only about $25,000, according to newspaper accounts.

"Cutler and his associates conspired ... to intentionally conceal the true owners of Tasman and ... to deceive and defraud," the legal documents filed by the CRC stated. The businessmen had wanted to keep their financial support of Tasman quiet to avoid retaliation from other quarry owners who were currently supplying both construction companies with stone.

Tasman disputed the allegations and noted that Johnson's interested had waned. Slavek, Cutler said, was only helping him out because Cutler was working in Australia. Pam Hickey, writing in *The*

Latrobe Bulletin of November 5, 1996, noted that "the most recent development in this series of allegations and claims is a rebuttal to the Tasman brief made by the conservancy. This brief reports, 'Although Tasman contends that the Conservancy's Motion blows matters out of proportion, the Conservancy maintains that intentional deception by a permit applicant is a serious matter.' The organization redefends its claim that Slavek is an unnamed owner and that the company has deliberately failed to follow the law."

The brief also noted, according to a *Tribune-Review* article on November 3, 1996, that Slavek expected to become an equity particpant in the quarry when it became operational. Johnson's interest ended in 1994, and he received nothing for his $200,000 investment, the article stated.

Getting Maggie Rosborough's legal case on the road reopened was a victory for us. And we weren't sure where the revelation about Tasman's real owner was headed, but we felt we were gaining ground. However, in the see-saw battle that was the quarry protest, just when a victory was attained for the good guys, the other side scored, too. Blairsville Municipal Authority had spent more than $120,000 in its efforts to battle the quarry. Hydrogeologist Jim Casselberry received more than $14,000. The engineering firm got more than $10,000, and the borough solicitor received over $5,000. Special consultants, Jones & Day, the Pittsburgh firm hired to fight the quarry, cost more than $69,000 in fees to the authority. All to have the firm turn around and get the BMA out of the lawsuit by entering into an agreement with Tasman to underwrite development of a water well which the authority could use as an alternate supply source. The well would be drilled regardless of whether Tasman's mining operations would affect the quality or quantity of surface and groundwater used by BMA.

When Jeff Himler filed that story in the December 27, 1996 *Blairsville Dispatch,* it was yet another end-of-year devastating blow for us. Both BMA and Tasman reserved the right to appeal any decisions of the DEP.

Tasman agreed to develop a new well, to pay for property rights for a new well, with the BMA to gain ownership of the well. BMA could provide input on the well's location. But Tasman could use the well to draw water for suppressing dust. A water monitoring agreement was made. Tasman also agreed to treat water discharges from the quarry to protect Trout Run, and to drill additional wells if the first replacement well didn't provide enough water for the BMA.

Tasman was the clear winner in this deal.

The money kept flowing, at a pace I knew the grotto could never have done. "Hi Ho, Hi Ho, It's Off To Court We Go!" was the headline of the latest Chestnut Ridge Conservancy newsletter. "At an estimated cost of $5,000 per day, the CRC hopes it isn't necessary to use all or more than the 26 days set aside for the hearing. The people who will be representing your concerns have spent over a year getting ready for these hearings. The CRC will be represented by an array of exceptional people:

"Law Firm—Klett, Lieber, Rooney, and Schorling

"Attorneys: Howard J. Wein Esq.—Environmental Counsel; Paul A. Supowitz, Esq.—Environmental Counsel.

"Board members: Russ Davies, MaryK Samios, Joanne Matthews, Maggie Rosborough, Byron Rodd, Dr. Joseph Merritt.

"Expert and Fact Witnesses: Dr. Robert Eppley—Water conduits/caves; Dr. Joseph Merritt—Mammalogist; John Hempel—Mining engineer and Hydrologist; Kim Opatka-Metzgar—Author, Caves and water sources; William Allen—Author, former Pittsburgh zoo supervisor of reptiles; Dr. Howard Reinert—herpetologist/threatened species; Dr. William Beimborn—wetlands delineation; David Shapira, property owner."

In preparation for the hearing, Paul Supowicz asked me to review a "Report of Dye-Tracing Study and Exploration of Copperhead Cave and Con Cave, Derry Township, Westmoreland County," written by DEP hydrogeologist D. Scott Jones. We prepared by phone, Paul going over what he would ask me, as well as what the opponents would grill me on.

Media attention on the hearings reminded me of all of the verbal sparring managers of professional boxers took part in. Attorney Steven F. Baicker-McKee for the opposition posed with a large-scale model of the proposed quarry for the *Tribune-Review*.

A sidebar article noted that Tasman Chief Executive Officer Clive Cutler had no plans to attend the lengthy proceedings.

"Nothing has changed," Harvey J. Eger, Tasman's attorney said, noting that Cutler planned to oversee operations from Australia. Tasman's counsel called Cutler well qualified to serve as president of Tasman, and denied that Cutler was serving as a front, something the conservancy suggested. Cutler, Eger said, had intened to remain in the United States throughout the life of the quarry, but was frustrated with the slow pace of the permit process and thus returned to Australia. He told the Tribune-Review that in his quarter-century in quarrying, he had never been through such an "exhaustive and extensive review process."

"Our experts believe incomplete and inaccurate information was provided to the department in this permit application," said Attorney Howard Wein.

"There are approximately 120 families in this residential community that will be affected by this quarry," said Dwayne Ross, representing the Hillside Community Association. "We're not asking for sympathy or pity; we are seeking the board's protection of their health and safety."

"This was not an easy permit to review," said Michael J. Heilman, assistant counsel with the DEP. He said "At DEP, when we make decisions, we do it right. We review all permit applications thoroughly."

Heilman said, "This was a huge permit. The department received a huge amount of correspondence regarding this permit. We received hundreds of letters, and responded to virtually all of them. This permit simply had to be done correctly, and we intend to show that it was."

"In no sense was there a 'rubber-stamping' of this permit," echoed Steven F. Baicker-McKee.

And along with all the attorneys and expert witnesses paraded before the Environmental Hearing Board, Chuck Hempel was there.

An expert on mining, mine permits, blasting, karst, geology, and any number of other issues, every time the other side turned around he was there. He was there sitting in a 70-year-old woman's Fayette County bedroom at 4 a.m. taking decibel readings of quarry trucks driving by her house, to counteract testimony from the other side on noise. He was there to visit nearly every limestone quarry site in southwestern Pennsylvania in his quest for data to use against the Chestnut Ridge Quarry. He devised fracture trace studies indicating the drainage patterns along the ridge. He missed not a day of testimony and spent hours before the hearings, at lunchtime, and after the hearings, planning strategy and gathering documentation for the protest.

During the environmental hearing, he was up at 6 a.m., home very late at night, and never seemed to sleep. His wife Jennifer recalled being awakened at 3 a.m. by his exclamation, "I've got them now. I've got the SOBs now." He was still at work.

The fight was a lot more to him than a consulting job. It meant saving the ridge, where he had first started caving over 30 years ago, where he and a lot of early Pittsburgh Grotto members cut their "caving teeth." To him, it was a 24-hour-a-day fight. During Rosborough's hearing on the road, an attorney for the mining company was surprised and probably a bit chagrined to see Chuck Hempel there as an expert witness.

"Surely you don't portray yourself as an expert on roads, too?" the attorney asked. Meanwhile, Chuck Hempel ticked off a list of cases involving roads where he had testified as an expert witness. The attorney was so dumbfounded he had no further questions. With Chuck Hempel's guidance, the DEP and Tasman Resources were hit again and again and again. The ship hadn't sunk yet, but it was damaged.

The Chestnut Ridge Conservancy, at the time of the hearing, had spent several hundred thousand dollars in its protest, and estimates are that the quarry operator and his backers spent well over two million. All due to a few thousand dollars and a lot of gumption and knowledge on the part of a little western Pennsylvania caving club.

But with all the evidence presented, even by the grotto, it seemed that nothing we had was enough to halt the quarry plan. The Chestnut Ridge Conservancy would gain a hearing, then lose a decision. Maggie Rosborough would plead her case, but to no avail.

Bob Eppley and I were scheduled to testify on the same day. As we drove down to Pittsburgh to the hearing room. I was a bit apprehensive, but Chuck Hempel was very reassuring. But the questioning pretty much followed my deposition, the opposing side continually coming at me trying to trip me up. Finally, they did, question after question coming so fast. They kept asking me to locate things on a topographic map which was so messed up with other scrawlings I could hardly locate things on it.

As we adjourned for lunch, Chuck pulled me aside and pointed out that one of the sites I had noted was off the permit area. We quickly corrected that in testimony after lunch, but our side couldn't afford any mistakes.

The testimony, which took an actual 30 days, set a record as the most days for a hearing before the EHB—ever. Testimony was completed in March, and then Judge Renwand was left to sift through nearly a month's worth of testimony and more than 20,000 pages of transcripts.

On April 30, 1997, we returned to the site with Judge Renwand, who wanted to examine many of the areas discussed in the testimony for himself.

"I came up here before the hearing began," Renwand told a newspaper reporter. "It gives me personal perspective on the area you just can't get from maps, photographs or videos."

Going along were Chuck Hempel, Scott Jones and staffers and members of the Department of Environmental Protection, Tasman Resources, and Chestnut Ridge Conservancy.

We met at the Shapira home in Fairfield Township and hiked up the ridge to look at water-flow monitoring points along Snyder's Run and its tributaries. The Shapira family had filed a civil suit against Tasman Resources alleging that Tasman wanted to discharge water illegally on their property, harming water, plants and animals there.

The visit was primarily to examine stream monitoring points and springs, and a property line/road issue in Hillside. The judge looked at some nearby limestone quarries two days later, and also met with Maggie Rosborough in Hillside.

"This haul road will be 75 feet from my front door," Maggie told the judge. "And it would carry 60,000 trucks a year."

The judge measured the width of the road near the railroad crossing, noting "two trucks couldn't even get through here side by side." Being thorough, he also went to see two other quarries in the area.

Then, with the conclusion of the hearings, we were back to waiting. And waiting. And waiting.

Chapter 17

Before I became a teenager, I was not allowed to go below the railroad tracks in Hillside unaccompanied by an adult. So, when I wanted to go bicycle riding with my friends, who lived below the railroad tracks, I would ride down the road and wait at the crossing until they came up to meet me.

Little did I know all those years later, how important the township road and the railroad crossing would be in trying to halt the quarry. The road issue was best summarized in an August 1998 brief in opposition to the variance request of Tasman Resources, Ltd., filed on behalf of the Hillside Community Association by Dwayne E. Ross, counsel for the HCA.

"Daniel Slavek, Jr., and his company, Derry Construction, under the guise of Tasman Resources, Ltd. has proposed to open a stone quarry atop the Chestnut Ridge lying partly in Derry Township and partly in Fairfield Township. In order to access this quarry to a township road, Tasman has proposed the construction of a road of approximately 2,500 feet in length. This proposed road will connect the haul road leading to and from the quarry with Township Road T-891. However, the construction of the road is not the problem. The problem is that Tasman must have this proposed road accepted by Derry Township as a public road. As conceded by Mr. Slavek at the hearing, they would not be able to use this proposed road as a haul road unless accepted by the Township as a public road due to the 300 feet buffer zone under the Department of Environmental Protection regulations. Specifically, this regulation prohibits any mining activity within 300 feet of any dwelling, unless waived by the homeowner(s). When Tasman realized they would be unable to obtain these waivers, they sought to circumvent this regulation by making part of the haul road a township road.

"Tasman's first step in making this road a township road was by entering into agreements with the Township relating to construction, dedication and acceptance of the proposed township road. These agreements were signed on December 29, 1993, the last business day before the newly-elected supervisors would take office. In these agreements, Township Ordinance 50 was modified. Ordinance 50 pertains to the Township requirements before any road is accepted. Despite the modification of an ordinance in these agreements, no notice was given to the public concerning these agreements nor was any action taken to accept Tasman's dedication at any monthly public meeting. The execution of these agreements took place at an unannounced special meeting before the end of the year. Once again, Tasman was taking whatever action was necessary to circumvent the law.

"On December 22, 1995, DEP granted to Tasman a mining permit for the stone quarry. The DEP relied upon the assertion of Tasman that the proposed road would be accepted as a township road. An appeal of this permit was promptly filed by Hillside Community Association to the Environmental Hearing Board. Before this permit was granted, there was discovered a discrepancy in the survey for this road and the adjacent property owned by Margaret and Jerry Rosborough and Martha Jones. In response to litigation involving this survey discrepancy, the Court of Common Pleas of Westmoreland County determined that Tasman owned only 40 feet and not 65 feet as set forth in their deed for the property along this proposed township road. Without the minimum 50 feet required by Township Ordinance 50, Tasman could not construct the proposed township road as set forth in the agreements."

But back to 1997. While we kept thinking of Pittsburgh and Judge Renwand's pending decision, the phones began ringing off the hook on June 19, when Westmoreland County Common Pleas Court Judge Daniel J. Ackerman ruled in favor of Maggie and Jerry Rosborough and Martha Jones after he had reopened their case. It was eighteen months after the permit was granted.

It had been seven years for us. Our first victory had been gained in 1995 when we had Copperhead Cave (Pennsylvania's 17th longest and third deepest cave) and the Trout Run area taken out of the mining permit. The permit was granted; however, the caves were saved.

In June of 1997, Judge Ackerman's ruling was a second victory, one potentially crippling blow to the whole quarry proposal. It was a long time coming, but Judge Ackerman determined that the access road the quarry planned would infringe upon the property of the Rosboroughs and Martha Jones.

Maggie Rosborough's lawsuit claimed that the original 1895 property survey gave her title to the land in question and that the proposed quarry haul road would use a right-of-way granted to neighboring properties but never intended for commercial use. The road would also encroach upon her land. Ackerman ruled that a right-of-way existed for the surrounding property owners, but stated that "the road proposed by Tasman, which it intends to dedicate to the township of Derry, would benefit lands not originally benefited by the easement over the Rosborough-Jones property, and specifically would benefit a proposed quarry three miles away, which would constitute an impermissible enlargement of the easement."

Ackerman upheld the survey Rosborough submitted making it impossible for the quarry company to encroach upon her land with the road they intended to dedicate to the township. That left Tasman with three other access options; however, none were improved roads and those would also have come very close to a number of homes. One road was the Firetower Road in Fairfield Township, which was already to be used as a temporary access road to the quarry. Steep, narrow and windy its use would pose a serious traffic danger to any vehicles traveling over it. The second option was the Millwood Hollow Road, a Derry Township road. Nothing more than a backwoods trail, it also would come too close to a number of houses in Millwood. The third option would be access to the property from the Derry Ridge Road, but the road issues were similar.

Tasman was given 90 days to come up with an alternative haul road plan.

By the summer of 1997 Tasman's patience was wearing thin. Dan Slavek, Jr., had been revealed as the secret owner of the business. He had a permit, but no easy way in our out of the site. Where cavers had been persistent, we weren't bringing up issues that would defeat the quarry. But Maggie Rosborough's persistence on the road issue, coupled with the Chestnut Ridge Conservancy's ability to raise money and take issues we had started and expand on them, was a lot to take. So it was understandable that Tasman's patience was pretty much non-existent.

In a letter dated November 12, 1997, on Tasman Resources stationery, Maggie Rosborough, the Hillside woman leading the battle to stop the quarry road, got quite a surprise. Signed by Daniel G. Slavek, Jr., who billed himself as "Co-ordinator of Tasman Resources Limited," the letter said:

"Dear Maggie,

"As a result of your statements and very astute 'news flashes' in the *Ligonier Echo,* Clive Cutler has appointed me, Daniel G. Slavek, Jr., as the head of his North American operations. In order to help defray the cost of his legal bills, incurred as a result of your protests to his quarry, Cutler has instructed me to make use of certain assets that he has in Hillside, Pa.

"The asset that he has referred to is 4.2 acres of highly valuable timber abutting you and Mrs. Martha Jones's property.

"After evaluating the situation, I propose to timber the property and transform the available land into a new business, the new business being a pig farm or for more colorful terminology, a 'swinette'.

"This new industry will be state of the art technology which will entail the use of recycled materials, e.g. wood slabs from the harvested timber, to contain the swine, and used truck bodies to house the above. This is all in keeping to Mr. Cutler's wishes to preserve the environment, conserve resources, and add to the 'pristine atmosphere' of your neighborhood.

"I hope that this letter brings you, Martha, Mr. Shapira, Elsie Hillman, MaryK. Samios, and the C.R.C. up to date on the latest events in Derry Township.

"Maggie, you have messed with Clive Cutler now you are 'messing with the best', Dan Slavek, Jr.

"If you have any questions, please call me at (number omitted).

"I would suggest that you contact the Westmoreland County Tax bureau to have your property reassessed at a lower rate. It is very evident to me and everyone else who has followed the newspaper that you purchased your current domicile as a means of personal financial gain. This was a very bad decision on your part and your supporters. Your so-called supporters who live in the privacy of Fox Chapel, Squirrel Hill and the Ligonier Valley.

"P.S. Wait for King Coal. This is another matter that will get you and your supporters' juices flowing."

Things didn't stop there. Martha Jones, who had sold Maggie and Jerry Rosborough the house at the center of the controversy, still lived nearby. She had a home as well as a rental home right at the entrance to Maggie's driveway and the controversial Tasman Road. Her stepson, Leonard, who was in favor of the quarry, lived in the center of the Hillside "loop," my parents across the road from him. Aside from being a co-plaintiff in Maggie and Jerry Rosborough's lawsuit, Martha became involved in a more personal way when a truck driven by her stepson allegedly struck her as it was trying to bring a piece of equipment onto the site of the future swinette.

Swinette sign erected by Dan Slavek above the railroad tracks in Hillside.

In testimony before Judge Ackerman, the Rosboroughs' attorney, James Rosenberg, elicited more details about Slavek's purpose in writing the letter to Maggie, and later, revealed information about the truck incident:

James Rosenberg: "Third paragraph, letter states, does it not, after evaluating the situation, I propose to timber the property and transform the available land into a new business, the new business being a pig farm or for more colorful terminology—quote—swinette—end quote, is that—

Dan Slavek: "Yes."

James Rosenberg: "Is that what it says?"

Dan Slavek: "Yes."

James Rosenberg: "And the word swinette, that is a word that you came up with?"

Dan Slavek: "Yes."

James Rosenberg: "And so, based upon Mr. Cutler's instructions to you to try and generate money on this property you decided to put a swinette on this property?"

Dan Slavek: "Either a swinette or use it for some other means."

James Rosenberg: "That is what the letter says?

Dan Slavek: "Yes. All right. That was a good idea of what I thought of."

James Rosenberg: "At that point you thought to send this letter to Ms. Rosborough had you ever done any investigation in terms of how much money a swinette would generate?"

Dan Slavek: "No."

In further questioning, Rosenberg brought out the fact that Slavek had sent another letter, not only to the Rosboroughs, but also to Judge Ackerman. "You indicate in that letter that you Dan Slavek, Jr., had lost over two million dollars as a result of fighting and trying to get that quarry put in?"

Dan Slavek: "Yes."

James Rosenberg: "So, this was now personal because it wasn't Tasman that had lost this money it was you personally who had lost over two million dollars?"

Dan Slavek: "Yes."

Slavek, Rosenberg contended, also hired Leonard Jones as a security guard for Derry Construction, although Slavek denied it.

James Rosenberg: "...you go see Mr. Jones Jr. at his house at least once a week and probably more than that?"

Dan Slavek: "I've never been to his house."

James Rosenberg: "You've been to his property, though?"

Dan Slavek: "Yes."

James Rosenberg: "And you talked to him on his property?"

Dan Slavek: "Yes."

James Rosenberg: "On a regular basis?"

Dan Slavek: "Every time I'm in the area."

James Rosenberg: "And you get records from him as to what is going on in that area?"

Dan Slavek: "Yes."

James Rosenberg: "And Mr. Jones Jr. on a nightly basis walks over to Tasman's property, stands on Tasman's property, which is fifty feet at most away from the front door of Ms. Rosborough's house and stands there and stares at the door until Ms. Rosborough comes home?"

Dan Slavek: "I don't know."

James Rosenberg: "He's never told you that?"

Dan Slavek: "No."

James Rosenberg: "And you're not aware that every evening Mr. Jones Jr. comes and stands on Tasman's property and says that he has

Tasman's permission to stand on the property and stare at the Rosborough's house?"

Dan Slavek: "No."

At the end of Harvey Eger's cross-examination, Judge Ackerman asked a question of the witness: "Mr. Slavek, you said that you acted out of frustration?

Dan Slavek: "Yes."

Judge Ackerman: "Are you ashamed of your actions?"

Dan Slavek: "To a certain extent yes."

To borrow a cliché, the newspapers had a field day with this. "Hillside Woman Engaged in 'Pig Battle' With Mining Company," was a headline in the *Blairsville Dispatch*. *The Dispatch* and *Tribune-Review* both printed Slavek's letter to Maggie Rosborough nearly word for word, the article by Dwayne Pickles quoting Maggie thus: "We aren't sure what his (Slavek's) intent was with this letter, whether it was a joke or a threat. But we are certainly discussing it with our attorney."

James Rosenberg went a step further, noting, "Obviously, we are appalled. We feel this is an attempt to intimidate a witness in an ongoing proceeding...My client will never be intimidated by Mr. Slavek or by Tasman. This (letter) only strengthens her resolve."

He said "this is all about a man and a company getting very desperate, and attempting to intimidate a witness. We take it to be a not-so-veiled threat against our client. They're trying to turn up the heat on her, but it won't be effective."

Maggie Rosborough, showing what she was made of, added, "We do feel that a 'swinette' would be more constructive use for the property than a haul road for a quarry."

Dan Slavek sent his second letter to attorneys, property owners, Judge Ackerman and a variety of people. It also appeared in local newspapers:

"Enough is enough. Appalled at the insinuation that I am the 'bad guy,' or the perpetrator of a grudge situation. This is strictly a business decision, not a vendetta, like the one that C.R.C. & Maggie has instituted.

"I, Daniel G. Slavek, Jr., President of Derry Construction Co. Inc., have invested nearly eight years of my time and $2,500,000 of my money in this project. You can realize by the above figures that this project was not conceived in an outhouse by candlelight.

"This has been a well-conceived plan to supply my firm, and hopefully other companies both large and small with stone at a competitive price and guaranteed supply.

"I am not a destroyer of the environment, as portrayed by the opposition. I am an employer of 150 hard working individuals, who are highly compensated for their efforts. These are not minimum wage jobs, e.g. a grocery store!

"I'm a firm believer that 'there is no gain without pain.' In this case, I have to know what mental, financial and emotional pain is really like. It is very disheartening to see what a few very vindictive self-serving people can create.

"Here Pennsylvania and Tom Ridge are trying to create jobs. These opponents are trying to destroy this. If you look at the big contributors to the C.R.C., you will see the supporters of the recently defeated 'stadium tax.'

"Other supporters of the C.R.C. are some of my suppliers. One of which has since refused to supply me, and the other who has openly admitted to giving Ms. Rosborough money in return for birthday cards and cookies.

"Now I know what I've got to do. A swinette is in order. 'Pork is the new white meat.'

"Sincerely,

"Daniel G. Slavek Jr.

"P.S. 'So many idiots, so few comments.' Well this letter expresses my comments! If you really want to dance with me, please turn on the music.

"cc: Harvey Eger, Esq., Chief Counsel to Tasman Resources; David Shapira, Giant Eagle; Elsie Hillman, Hillman Cos.; Scott Roberts, DEP; Rosenberg, Marcus & Shapira; Howard Wein; Floyd Ganassi; Judge Ackerman; Josh Whetzel; MaryK Samios; Martha Jones; Maggie Rosborough.

"These names are listed in the order of their importance."

Another Dwayne Pickels article in the *Tribune-Review* had the headline "Quarry 'soap opera' going to the pigs. Each side maintains the other is letting dispute turn into the vendetta."

Pickels' story dealt with Slavek's second letter, Slavek telling the reporter that his asphalt plant at Davison Sand and Gravel Co.'s Torrance site was idled because local suppliers refused to provide stone for him. Slavek reported that his asphalt plant was a million dollar investment sitting idle because getting stone through commercial sources was expensive. He said his company used about a half million tons a year for asphalt and road construction.

"Maybe he stands to lose $2.5 million, but it's not our fault," Maggie Rosborough said. "Had he listened to us years ago, he might not be in this position. We have asked (Tasman) to find an alternate route and spare Hillside, but they totally disregarded our concerns and went full force with their plans."

Dan Slavek granted an exclusive interview with *The Latrobe Bulletin* on November 24, 1997, continuing his public relations campaign that the quarry would bring more jobs, good-paying jobs, to the area, and talking about his efforts to comply with all the requests made of him.

"When the Hillside Community Association and Chestnut Ridge Conservancy started fighting the quarry, I complied with every one of their demands except one," Slavek said. "That is, I will not let either of those groups dictate the hours the quarry will operate. Other than that, what they wanted, they got."

The Bulletin also interviewed a Hillside resident who favored the quarry, Leonard Jones, Jr., the stepson of Martha Jones, who was part of Maggie and Jerry Rosborough's lawsuit regarding the road.

"He noted that he grew up in the house Rosborough now lives in," wrote staff writer Jeannette Wolff. 'My stepmother had that house for sale for $130,000, but lowered the price to $86,000 for Maggie. She said she did it because Maggie was an activist and would fight the quarry.

"'Maggie, on the other hand, testified at the DEP hearing that she didn't know anything about the quarry until a week after purchasing her home in April 1995, even though a public information session was held about the quarry in December 1994.'

Jones told the newspaper that "the right of way to Maggie's house isn't on her deed. It was a separate one that my stepmother still held after the sale. When it looked like that right of way was the way to stop the quarry, Maggie and her husband bought half of it.

"'Maggie claimed she was buying the right of way because she was worried about access to her property in the future. That's interesting because there is about a half-mile she has to travel between her property and the right of way that is owned by someone else. Buying that right of way didn't assure her of anything except a way to fight Tasman.'"

Jones even went so far as to accuse Maggie Rosborough and his stepmother of preventing people from using the road. "She and my stepmother would not allow anyone to use the road. They would run out there and chase people off if they were on it. The bad part of that was that there are two houses below Maggie and those people needed to use the right of way."

Jones said "Maggie opposes the quarry on the grounds it would be a safety threat, but she forced two families to drive along the side of the railroad tracks to get to their homes. Steve Havash was on his way up to visit one of the Lenhart kids the day he was hit and killed by a train. If Martha and Maggie had allowed people on that right of way at that time, he wouldn't have had to be down at the tracks."

Jones was referring to a local teenager who was killed in February of 1997 while riding an all-terrain vehicle along the railroad tracks with another teen. State police reported that Matthew Stephen Havash, 15, apparently steered the vehicle into the train's path. Conrail officials told the *Tribune-Review* that the boy apparently "lost control of the vehicle and it flipped over, propelling him beneath the train."

However, the war of the words got a little carried away, and *The Bulletin* was forced to print a retraction due to the unsubstantiated claims. The front page retraction noted that "an article in Monday's Bulletin concerning the proposed Hillside quarry contained questions expressing opinions that should not be construed as actual verified facts.

"The opinions of Leonard Jones as expressed to questions in the article are entirely denied by Maggie Rosborough. In particular, Rosborough denied Jones' allegation that she has denied her neighbors access to a right of way on her property and was in any way responsible for the death of a child along the adjacent railroad tracks. Neighbors state that Rosborough has not prevented them from using the right of way. That information should have been included in the article. The story was published without complete investigation into the circumstances concerning that tragic accident, and the *Bulletin* apologizes for any incorrect implication that Rosborough and/or Martha Jones had any involvement in the accident."

Maggie Rosborough, not one to take things sitting down in the war of words, later gained the attention of *Pit & Quarry* magazine, an article entitled "Hogging attention" appearing in the April, 1998, issue, complete with photo of the swinette sign.

"Road safety, air quality, noise pollution, water table levels, endangered animal and plant species, historic caves, an old graveyard and scenic views are all under scrutiny. The neighbors maintain that if Slavek had been a little more direct in his dealings, the court fights and bruising public debate would not be necessary," wrote James E. Guyette.

"'Maybe he should have taken us seriously,' says neighbor Maggie Rosborough, who opposes the venture with the Chestnut Ridge Conservancy. 'He should have listened to us and worked with us. We tried to make this a win-win situation.'

"Rosborough and neighbors are most formidable opponents. Rosborough is a walking media sound bite with a dead-on style of delivery laced with dead-pan humor. They've printed up t-shirts, hired lawyers and called in the press.

"'We've tried to get as much media coverage of this as possible,' she notes. The local papers keep churning out stacks of stories with headlines such as 'Pig farm escalates quarry quarrel.'"

The magazine noted that Slavek was less than forthcoming for its article and noted the point of controversy about Slavek's alleged arranging to have a township supervisor vote in favor of the haul road on the supervisor's last day in office.

"'He could have done this and not created the alarm that he did,' says Rosborough, who notes that required legal notices were placed in a newspaper not read by residents in that immediate area. 'They were kept totally in the dark,' she says. Tasman 'felt no obligation to notify anyone.'

The article concluded that "Rosborough continues to score points in public opinion because she refuses to be an opponent to mining and other progress-type endeavors. 'Quarries help build roads and build communities,' she declares. 'I think quarrying is a decent and honorable profession, but I feel he (Slavek) has done a disfavor to the quarry industry as a whole.'"

Leonard Jones, Jr., was also to resurface in the quarry battle, when he was accused of striking his stepmother with a truck in yet another argument over the right of way/road. The incident with Martha Jones also became part of the testimony considered by Judge Ackerman in the roadway case against Tasman. Samuel Matovic of Ligonier, an employee of Derry Construction, testified on February 4, 1998. He was driving the truck on Thursday, January 15, 1998, taking a highlift "to the quarry property that is—swinette—there."

Matovic testified that as he was driving his truck to the right of way, a car appeared in front of the truck in the driveway. He identified Martha Jones and a Mrs. Clark. "So they stayed in front of the truck on the edge of the road. So I backed up and I—Leonard Jones was with me. And he said go down through the grassy area. So I backed the truck up and went down the—in front of the truck again."

"This was then down on the grassy area away from the gravel road?" asked Harvey Eger, attorney for Tasman.

"Yes," Matovic answered. "It was Leonard Jones told me that is the right of way.... They was stopped in front of me and I said this isn't right."

"What do you mean?" Eger asked.

"Them standing out in front of the truck like that trying to stop—you know I never step out in front of a truck...So, Leonard said, keep going. I said I can't. This is not right. I got out of the truck and he got out of the truck. He said I'll take the truck down, you know. I said you can't go down through there. He said I will. So he started nudging the truck forward and well in the meantime Mrs. Clark went inside and called the state police. And Mrs. Jones is standing out in front of the truck. He kept nudging and she had her hand like in front of the bumper and she fell down. I said Leonard she's under the steering tire, she's lying under the steering tire. So I got out and he pushed her foot aside and he pushed it back. And in the meantime we can't do nothing, waited until the ambulance came. And two ambulances and I guess two or three fire trucks came and checked her over, picked her up, put her in the ambulance."

James Rosenberg, attorney for the Rosboroughs and Martha Jones, elicited more details of the incident: "And then Mr. Jones got into the driver's seat?"

"He said I'll take the truck out."

"And then he started driving the truck down on the grass and off the gravel road?"

"He was in the grass, yes."

"And he kept driving the truck as Mrs. Jones was backing up?"

"Well, she didn't back up too far. She held her hand on the bumper and then she fell down."

"And there were ruts that were put into the grass that are approximately fifty feet long, aren't there?"

"After she was on the ground, yes, she was in the ambulance."

"And Mrs. Jones was backing up and Mr. Jones came—kept driving the truck towards her?"

"Until she fell down."

Jones was charged with recklessly endangering another person and simple assault, and was accepted into Accelerated Rehabilitation Disposition for nine months.

Never a dull moment.

Chapter 18

During the course of the quarry protest, it had been in my mind for a number of years that while protesting was able to save the caves of the Chestnut Ridge, there had to be something more which could be done, a better way to protect and preserve caves. I had been talking to a number of cavers about it, and by November of 1997, eleven of us gathered together to form the Mid-Atlantic Karst Conservancy. If we could buy caves, own them, then we could certainly see to their future, see that caves were protected, conserved.

We approved bylaws, a constitution, and began the process of incorporating as a 501(c)3 corporation. We began targeting properties to acquire and were busy with the business of the conservancy.

After the road decision, the word testimony once again became part of our lives, as amidst all of our conservancy work, we were among 75 people who attended a hearing held by DEP on the quarry's air quality permit. Air quality issues were supposedly reviewed by DEP as part of its original mining permit review, but legal pressure and arguments put forward by the Chestnut Ridge Conservancy caused the air permit to evolve into a separate and significant permit requirement for Tasman.

"The requirements placed on the processing and hauling operations have significantly broadened as a result of the pressure exerted by the CRC and will require Tasman to meet stringent standards before an air permit can be issued," the conservancy newsletter stated. "The decision to separate the two issues, although more costly in the litigation arena, is not only a vindication of the position of the CRC, that all air issues must be considered together, but also provides a second appeal opportunity if necessary."

The Bureau of Air Quality conducted the hearing. Maggie Rosborough, once again on top of the issues, noted the "'waste of taxpayers dollars' in proceeding with Tasman's permit, since the haul road through Hillside outlined on DEP maps 'does not exist.'"

Since the air quality permit application must be accurate and complete, she argued, "You can't use the excuse that you don't know that the road is not okay."

Bill Charlton of DEP admitted that if there was a substantial change in the configuration or location of the road it would require a new air quality permit.

Howard Wein, CRC attorney, brought up the infamous "swinette" letter. The conservancy also had its own air quality expert, and issues such as dust, water reserves for dust control, and pollution were also argued.

In February of 1998, Dan Slavek continued his letter-writing, this time taking out a full page ad in *The Latrobe Bulletin,* as an "open letter to the residents of the Derry Area."

"I have been portrayed by those against the quarry as a money-hungry, uncaring predator attempting to rape and pillage the natural beauty of the area; as someone unconcerned about the health and safety of my neighbors," the letter said. "In an effort to counter that misconception, I have agreed to protective measures for the residents and the environment at Tasman Quarry that are far beyond any that were ever required of my nearby competitors.

"Still, it wasn't enough. As a further show of good faith, I recently offered to give one percent of the quarry's total gross revenue back to the township in the form of a donation each year to the township fire companies and the Derry Area Recreation Board.

"In exchange, I asked the township to give Tasman Quarry an easement to the required 50-foot right of way. To date, the township supervisors have refused to acknowledge or act upon my proposal. In response to my offer, some township residents have accused me of trying to bribe them. Nothing could be further from the truth. I am confident that the Westmoreland County courts will eventually clear the way for the quarry to proceed—with or without my one percent donation.

"I hoped the possibility of a donation that could generate sums in the area of $70,000 per year would hasten an end to the hard feelings. To insure that my donation is seen in the light I intended it, I want to state that when the quarry is operational, I will give the township one percent of its revenue, whether it operates with the township's blessing or by court order.

"Anyone who views my offer as a bribe should look at what I already donate to this area with nothing expected in return. "

Citing his civic works in the area, Slavek concluded by offering "to sit down with those opposed to the quarry and discuss the compromises I am willing to make. They include being willing to build a fenced playground on property I own in Hillside instead of the pig farm I had announced I will build. I am also willing to put a member of the Hillside Community Association, of the association's choosing, on the board that will administer my one percent donation to the township. What compromises are you willing to make to end the fighting?"

"You sound like a desperate man to get what you want at our expense," Hillside resident Joyce Spangler wrote in a letter to the editor responding to Slavek's advertisement. "Actions do speak louder than words. Your actions don't coincide with your open letter."

I got into the letter writing act, and penned this missive to *The Latrobe Bulletin:*

"Dan Slavek's latest proposal for the Tasman Resources Quarry on Chestnut Ridge sounds like the same old Tasman rhetoric:

"Tasman statement: In August of 1992 Clive Cutler of Tasman told Derry Township supervisors the quarry would last 25 years. *(Tribune-Review,* Aug. 27, 1992) Fact: After being confronted with copies of courthouse documents at a township meeting, he admitted the full length of the quarry would be 50 years (*Blairsville Dispatch*, Sept. 10, 1992, Westmoreland County Deed Book 2069, page 021).

"Tasman statement: In its permit application (Module 7, Hydrology), Tasman stated that there were no wetlands on the SMT Family Partnership site that were within 1,000 feet of the permit area. Fact: During the site visits at least four wetlands sites were indicated by witnesses.

"Tasman statement: In 1992 Tasman's 'experts' reported no signs of the eastern woodrat, a threatened species, on any of the property in the mining permit. (Eastern Woodrat [*Neotoma Floridana*] Survey at Site of the Proposed Chestnut Ridge Quarry in Derry Township, Tasman Resources, Ltd.) Fact: There were 34 Woodrat sites identified by Loyalhanna Grotto in its response to the permit application, through photographic evidence and maps presented to the Department of Environmental Protection (*Report on Deficiencies in the Chestnut Ridge Quarry Application of Tasman Resources, Limited, Derry and Fairfield Townships, Westmoreland County, Pennsylvania*).

"Tasman statement: In its quarry application, Tasman indicated there were no endangered or rare plants on the property. Fact: During the environmental hearing, renowned expert Dr. William Beinborn testified to the presence of *thalictrum corialeum*, the thickleafed meadow rue at five different locales in the permit area. The meadow rue is a threatened plant located on the very limestone Tasman is proposing to mine.

"Tasman statement: Tasman's initial quarry proposal (*Historical Resources Determination Notice,* quarry permit application) indicated there were no historic sites on the SMT Family partnership land. Fact: In 1994 the Loyalhanna Grotto and local residents pointed out seven historic homesteads and the Burry cemetery, providing photographs of the homestead sites to DEP. (*Report on the Deficienciesi n the Chestnut Ridge Quarry Application of Tasman Resources, Limited, Derry and Fairfield Townships, Westmoreland County, Pennsylvania*).

"Fact: In its permit application Tasman said it had a legal, 50-foot-wide right of way to connect the SMT Family Partnership Property in Hillside to a township road at the railroad tracks. Fact: On June 19, 1997, Judge Daniel Ackerman of the Westmoreland County Court of Common Pleas ruled otherwise. Ackerman ruled part of the right of way Tasman claimed was on the property of Maggie and Jerry Rosborough and Martha Jones.

"This small sampling of Tasman statements and the subsequent facts presented by groups like the Chestnut Ridge Conservancy, Loyalhanna Grotto and the Hillside Community Association (HCA) all seem to be forgotten. We need a reminder. This isn't just about a business venture. This is about damage to watersheds, to wetlands, to endangered, rare and threatened plants and animals, to air quality and of the safety of the community of Hillside, not protests by a bunch of not-in-my-backyard residents who are only concerned with themselves.

"Tasman statement: Just a few months ago Dan Slavek wrote a letter to the editor of *The Latrobe Bulletin* claiming he had no personal interest in the Tasman quarry: 'I have no financial reason or motive for writing this letter except for the betterment of Derry Township in general. ... I am not using this as a public forum to get into politics in Derry Township for personal gain.' (Jan. 2, 1996). Module 3 of the permit application never mentions his name. Fact: Now he is the North American representative for the company who has invested over $2.5 million in the venture (*Post-Gazette,* Nov. 30,

1997).

"Tasman statement, regarding the proposed pig farm it plans to install next to the Rosboroughs' and Jones' homes: 'This is strictly a business decision, not a vendetta, like the one CRC and (Rosborough) have instituted—Dan Slavek Jr. (*Tribune-Review*, Nov. 28, 1997). Fact: If it is not a vendetta, why does the sign Slavek has erected in Hillside state 'Future site of the Hillside Swinette. Courtesy of the CRC'?

"Tasman statement: During testimony before the (DEP) on Dec. 20, 1994, Clive Cutler Testified that there would be an average of 80 loads per day leaving the quarry site. Now Dan Slavek (*Latrobe Bulletin,* Dec. 11, 1997) is promising one percent of the revenues from Tasman's quarry to aid local fire departments and a recreation board. The $7 million used as an annual estimate for the $70,000 in revenues to be donated would be transported by 80 trucks a day?

"Remember Tasman's many statements: Consider the source."

The months passed, then a spring day in March, 1998, I got home from work to see a light blinking on my answering machine. It was a message from Jennifer Hempel to call her right away. I dialed, my hands shaking, wondering if it was over. I don't remember what was said, only my heart nearly jumping out of my chest as she told me the news. Judge Renwand of the Environmental Hearing Board had issued his ruling. We had won! Tears flowed freely down my cheeks. As I hung up, alone in the house, scaring the dog, but not caring, I let out a whoop that could probably be heard a mile away.

"It's over. We won. Tell everyone," I said as I called my sister, repeating myself because she couldn't comprehend what I told her through my tears the first time. I remember a basketball game in high school when our winless team was down by one point with eight seconds left. We were in the bonus and I was fouled. I made the first, then the second, and the opponent's last-minute shot fell short as my coaches and teammates and probably some of the fans crowded onto the court, jumping up and down, shouting and hugging. That blinking red light, that phone call—it was better than winning that game—it was like winning the lottery.

I don't remember whom I called in what order, but there was Maggie Rosborough, my parents, my grandmother, Tom, Bob Eppley.

"When the permittee fails to demonstrate that it has a legal means of accessing its permit site from a township road, the Department erred in granting the permit," the judge's opinion and order stated, noting that the "proposed public road, although it will serve as an extension to the haul road, is not covered by the permit since it is to be constructed outside the physical boundaries of the permit. It is the contention of the Appellants that Tasman, by treating the proposed township road as separate from the permitted haul road, sought to circumvent the setback requirements of the noncoal mining regulations...Because the proposed road would be within 300 feet [75 by measurement of Maggie Rosborough] of an occupied dwelling, without the owner's consent it would not meet the setback requirements of the regulations."

The judge noted that a township supervisor testified that the agreement had not been signed at a regularly scheduled meeting of the supervisors and the appropriate advertising requirements had not been completed. Judge Renwand included a brief history of Tasman's attempts to develop the access road, however, "nearly nine months have passed since the Board stayed this matter so that Tasman could submit to the Department a new proposal for access to and egress from its mine site. Nearly one year has passed since the conclusion of the hearing on this appeal. More than two years have passed since this permit was issued. Tasman has agreed not to commence its operation until the access issue is resolved. At present, the issue of access to and from the mine site appears no closer to resolution than it did nine months ago. As the situation currently stands, Tasman holds a permit for a mine site which it cannot access or exit for the purpose of mining limestone.

"At the hearing on the merits, the Department's lead permit reviewer was asked, 'What happens if Tasman is unable to build (the proposed road)?' He responded that Tasman 'will have no other access to the public highway authorized from the haul road in the permit."

Citing various legal opinions on access roads and the law regarding noncoal surface mining permits, Judge Renwand noted that it is not the Department's role to rule on ownership or access. However, he noted that "in the present case, the Department issued a permit for a limestone quarry that had no means of access to a public road... At the time it approved the permit, the Department was aware of a dispute concerning Tasman's easement and whether Tasman had a legitimate right to build the roadway as proposed. Nevertheless, the Department approved the permit without further consideration of this matter. The Department's failure to further examine this matter and to build a record insuring that the requirements of the Noncoal Mining Act and regulations were satisfied constitutes an abuse of discretion."

Normally, the judge wrote, the Environmental Hearing Board would remand the permit to the Department, but as Tasman had more than three years to develop access, and because Tasman has been unsuccessful, "there does not appear to be a resolution to this matter in the very near future. In the meantime, Tasman holds a permit for a mine site it cannot access or exit, and the Appellants are given no finality in their appeal. Remanding the matter to the Department would not change this status; we, therefore, decline to do so. ... In light of these considerations, we find it appropriate to grant the Appellants' Motion to Sustain Appeal. The following order is entered:

"...AND NOW, this 26th day of March, 1998, the Motion to Sustain Appeal filed by the Appellants in this matter is granted. The permit which is the subject of this appeal is hereby revoked."

"It's pretty fundamental that in order to mine, a company has to have a way in and out of the mine site," Attorney Howard Wein said. "Since Tasman didn't, the judge did the right thing in revoking the permit."

He added that "It has always been the desire of the conservancy members to protect the area, which contains 40 caves, the endangered woodrat, timber rattlesnakes, and is a beautiful ridge. They've approached the owner to try to buy the site but have been rebuffed."

"Obviously we are elated," MaryK Samios told *Tribune-Review* staff writer Dwayne Pickels. She said it had been a long, hard battle and the ruling was a great relief to everyone who was a member of the Chestnut Ridge Conservancy. She said conservancy members felt vindicated. "This shows us justice is still out there...the system does work."

"This is certainly a giant step for Hillside," the HCA's attorney, Dwayne Ross, said. "But I'm sure it's not the last nail in the coffin."

"The judge relied on extraneous facts, many of which were not even accurate," Attorney Stephen F. Baicker-McKee stated, noting he would probably appeal the decision to Commonwealth Court. He said the road issue was beyond the EHB's jurisdiction.

Words could hardly express our feelings on the victory. As I got the message out to cavers, I wrote:

"In a long-awaited decision, Environmental Hearing Board Judge

Thomas Renwand on Thursday, March 26, 1998, revoked all permits for the proposed Tasman Resources, Ltd., Chestnut Ridge Quarry, sustaining the appeal filed by the Chestnut Ridge Conservancy and the Hillside Community Association over the Department of Environmental Protection's issuance of the mining permit.

'Judge Renwand's decision was based primarily on the road issue. A ruling was issued in that case by Judge Ackerman in favor of property owners Maggie and Jerry Rosborough and Martha Jones, who filed suit against Tasman over the proposed right-of-way for the quarry. Tasman, Judge Ackerman ruled, did not have the required 50-foot right-of-way for the road.

"Judge Renwand, in his ruling, issued after a record 31 days of testimony last winter, noted that the access for quarry trucks was indeed pertinent to the quarry permit (the quarry proponents said it was not), and revoked DEP's issuance of the permit. What this means, in simple language, is that Tasman lost its permit to mine Loyalhanna limestone on top of Chestnut Ridge.

"Tasman had already appealed Judge Ackerman's decision on the road to Commonwealth Court, and has the option of appealing Judge Renwand and the Environmental Hearing Board's decision to the state Superior Court. It's not over yet, but revocation of the permit is a major step in finally ending the eight-year battle to stop the quarry and to protect Copperhead Cave and the Blairsville Borough watershed.

"Grotto members Bob Eppley, Kim Metzgar and Chuck Hempel testified before the Environmental Hearing Board on the side of the Chestnut Ridge Conservancy and the Hillside Community Association last spring.

"What's next we don't know. We don't know what the landowner, the SMT Family Partnership, will do now. We don't know whether Tasman Resources will file another permit application (and waste more millions of dollars). We don't know if the court rulings in our favor will be overturned. We do know that right now Tasman has no mining permit. We do know that Tasman has no right-of-way. And we do know that thanks to Chuck Hempel and Maggie Rosborough and the Chestnut Ridge Conservancy, nothing will be going on in this area (mining-wise) for a long time. Some of the notes we got, via the grotto's email network, include the following comments:

"'Thank you and all the people who participated in this effort. I have been holding my breath over this for many years. Now I can let loose with at least one sigh of relief. I never thought it would go this far...but now it should be ended—unless SMT finally agrees to sell the land and rights to a conservation organization. Hmmmmm!!!!'"

"'It is 4 a.m. and that is the best news I have heard all night. Thanks for leaving a message.'"

"'There's dancing in the aisles here. I wonder what they will do with the property now that it's not useful to them anymore? They are just the sort of people who would dynamite all the caves shut and pollute the groundwater. I hope that doesn't happen for the town's sake as well as the bats. I'm glad there's people like you, Bob and Chuck in the world. It gives me hope that there'll be something left to pass on to my children.'"

"'Well, what now? Does this mean that Uncle Vic will not find it cost effective to have the hillside patrolled anymore, and that over the next couple of years things will revert back to pre-1990 status. It's a nice thought, but there's probably way too much bad blood to ever see open access to the land again. Hell, I can seem him continuing to pay for security just to spite everybody. I know I would love to be able to do Con Cave and Copperhead again. Dream on Whiteboy!'"

While Bear Cave remained open throughout the quarry protest, we breathed a sigh of relief that this historic cave, one of the longest in Pennsylvania, would be protected forever when the quarry permit was overturned. Below, Tom in Bear Cave.

One Voice

Chapter 19

Tasman Resources made its appeal of Judge Renwand's ruling less than a month later, on April 24. There were a dozen objections:

"(a) The EHB erred in its ruling by relying on facts not contained within the EHB record;

"(b) The EHB erred in its ruling by relying on factual developments that occurred after issuance of Tasman's Noncoal Permit;

"(c) The EHB erred in its ruling by finding that the DEP abused its discretion due to its alleged failure to investigate and compile a record on an issue and/or evidence that had not developed or been presented to DEP at the time of permit issuance;

"(d) The EHB erred in its ruling by speculating about future events;

"(e) The EHB erred in its ruling by relying on factual inaccuracies;

"(f) The EHB erred in its ruling because the decision is inconsistent with its opinion in Coolspring Stone Supply, Inc. v. DEP, Docket No. 96-171-R (March 25, 1998), which the EHB issued just one day before its Order in the instant case, and other EHB precedent;

"(g) The EHB erred in its ruling because the property subject to the dispute is located outside of the permitted property; the property subject to the dispute is not adjacent to the permitted property; and neither the Permit nor the Noncoal Act, pursuant to which DEP issued the Permit, address property or roads lying beyond the permitted property.

"(h) The EHB erred in its ruling because it revoked, rather than remanded, Tasman's Noncoal Permit;

"(i) The EHB erred in its ruling because its Order rests on a legal ground or factual finding which was not proposed by any party in the Motion to Sustain Appeal;

"(j) The EHB erred in its ruling by failing to cite or otherwise rely upon any regulation or statute as the basis for its ruling or its finding that the DEP abused its discretion;

"(k) The EHB erred in its ruling by failing to articulate and provide guidance to the regulated community and the DEP regarding standards for application, review, and issuance of permits pursuant to the Noncoal Act;

"(l) The EHB committed reversible error by rendering a decision that unnecessarily and unfairly permanently extinguishes Tasman's Noncoal Permit, violating fundamental principles of equity and the laws and Constitution of the Commonwealth.

"WHEREFORE, Petitioner Tasman Resources, Ltd. Prays the Court to reverse the March 26, 1998 Order of the Environmental Hearing Board, and remand the case to the Board for further proceedings consistent with this Court's Order."

It took only three days for Judge Renwand to deny the Motion for Oral Argument En Banc. He wrote: "Reconsideration is within the discretion of the Board and will be granted only for compelling and persuasive reasons. 25 Pa. Code 1021.124 (a). These reasons may include the following:

"(1) The final order rests on a legal ground or a factual finding which has not been proposed by any party.

"(2) The crucial facts set forth in the petition.

"(i) Are inconsistent with the findings of the Board.

"(ii) Are such as would justify a reversal of the Board's decision.

"(iii) Could not have been presented earlier to the Board with the exercise of due diligence.

"Neither Tasman nor the Department have set forth any grounds which would warrant reconsideration of our March 26, 1998 Opinion and Order. The issues set forth in the petitions are either untimely or have already been addressed in the Opinion itself. Therefore, reconsideration is denied. However, we feel it is important to address certain allegations and mischaracterizations contained in the petitions and supporting memoranda so that the record is clear."

The judge wrote that:

•The board did not rely solely on information which was not available to the Department at the time it conducted the permit review.

•The appellants stated that the roadway issue was not raised until after the permit was issued. However, Maggie Rosborough's testimony (Notes of Testimony, p. 2290) made evident that the issue was brought forward before the permit was issued. He cited letters and facsimiles in the Department's review file as well: "The fact that a large number of complaints are filed during the course of a permit review does not necessarily lessen the importance or impact of an individual complaint. This is especially true here where the individual letter raises a question as to whether the permit applicant has a sufficient legal interest in the property on which it intends to construct an extension to its haul road. Moreover, while Mrs. Rosborough's November 14, 1995 telefax may have been only one of over 900 letters received by the Department regarding the Tasman application, according to her testimony and affidavit her letter was sent in conjunction with numerous telephone calls made to the Department."

•The Judge noted that it was within the Department's duty to evaluate property-related issues and contracts for the purpose of determining compliance with regulations and statutes.

•Tasman had argued that "because the disputed property is outside the permit boundaries, this issue is outside the Department's jurisdiction and outside the scope of the Board's review...A simple declaration by the Department or permittee that a portion of a surface mining operation is 'outside' the permit boundaries does not necessarily make it so."

•"Tasman and the Department argue that the Board should not have revoked the permit but, instead, should have remanded the matter to the Department for further consideration. As noted in our Opinion, remand is not always the best course of action. Here, it would be fruitless since there is no meaningful course of action the Department can take."

•"The Department asserts that we should remand this matter so that it may take further action, presumably to provide Tasman with an opportunity to review other options. However, the evidence presented at the hearing by the Department established that if Tasman could not build the proposed roadway, there was no other feasible means of access to the site...We are not required to stay this matter indefinitely to allow Tasman time to consider and develop other proposals. The appropriate time for considering various proposals and options is prior to the permit issuance."

•"Finally, the petitions for reconsideration appear to imply that, were it not for our finding that the Department should have considered the property dispute issue, we would have upheld the permit. The issue of the property dispute was just one of many issues the Appellants raised in their appeal. Had we not granted the Appellants' Motion to Sustain Appeal, we would have continued with the briefing schedule which was stayed at the request of the parties following the ruling by the Westmoreland County Court of Common Pleas and we would have proceeded to adjudicate the other issues raised by the Appellants. Because Tasman and the Department have not demonstrated any grounds for reconsideration, their petitions are denied."

But of course, that wasn't the end of it. Tasman appealed to Commonwealth Court. And why make one appeal, when you can make more than one? Tasman then appealed Judge Ackerman's decision on the road to the state Superior Court. In July that appeal was denied.

In the meantime, Tasman had also filed suit against Derry Township, seeking a declaratory judgment to force the township to accept its proposed road in Hillside. Judge Daniel Ackerman, who ruled in favor of Maggie Rosborough, wrote that "If Tasman is to receive approval for a right of way, a portion of which is less than 50 feet wide, it must be obtained by following the procedural provisions of the Second Class Township Code, rather than by private agreement."

In May of 1998 the supervisors announced a public hearing on the road issue. The hearing ended up having three sessions, on June 16, July 14 and July 29. Maggie and Jerry Rosborough and Martha Jones were represented by their attorney, Jim Rosenberg, and Hillside residents turned out in full force. The same issues were argued, with Dan Slavek noting that if the appeal on the road is unsuccessful, it would mean the end of the quarry plan. Even Chuck Hempel got into the fray, testifying about traffic and safety issues.

It would be a few months until supervisors announced their decision; however, in the meantime, SMT Family Partnership got into the letter-writing campaign, taking out a quarter-page advertisement as an open letter to the township supervisors in *The Latrobe Bulletin.* Signed by Victor P. Smith, Jr., he wrote:

"SMT Family Partnership owns over 5500 acres in Derry Township and is perhaps the largest individual private real estate owner in the township. In one form or another, we have owned property in Derry Township for more than fifty years and, in that time, thousands of others have with and without our permission used and enjoyed our land without any compensation or benefit to SMT.

"In fact, the opposite is true, especially in the case of our 4800 acre Chestnut Ridge parcel. Besides the enormous sums of money involved in acquiring this property there is the tens of thousands of dollars required every year in the form of taxes, insurance, upkeep and maintenance. Not to mention the additional cost of cleaning up the tons of garbage illegally dumped there every year; repairing the thousands of dollars of vandalism done by ignorant individuals every year, defending ridiculous unfounded law suits brought on by trespassers looking to make a quick buck from an insurance settlement; patrolling the property during hunting season to keep the property safe and the game population in check; or the medical care for a guard who is almost killed by a irate trespasser trying to intentionally run him over.

"SMT and their family members have been verbally and physically threatened. We've had fists and guns pointed at us while being told what others are going to do on our property whether we like it or not. We've paid our dues and have earned the right to own property in Derry Township.

"Now we face the threat of deep-pocketed individuals of money and influence hiding behind the façade of so-called conservation groups and other narrow-minded, self-serving individuals who have their share of the American Dream and don't want anyone else to have his and who have continued to spread lies and misinformation regarding this property and the property development.

"The time has come when SMT can no longer afford to own this property without developing all the opportunities and recovering any and all economic benefits within our rights. This includes, however unpopular, the right to legally remove the natural resources and develop the remaining property in any manner available.

"The Derry Township supervisors must look beyond what's popular or what people of influence are asking and see this request for what it is. A simple request to vary the requirements when for all intensive [sic] purposes the letter of the law has been met and there are no alternative means to do otherwise. The use of this road is not the issue and should not be part of the decision. This road like all public roads will serve no single purpose and be used by the public to serve many different needs.

"If this variance is denied then there can never again be a variance approved in Derry Township for if this case doesn't meet the perimeters [sic] required to approve a variance provided for by law then no other request could possibly meet them in the future.

"By not approving the requested variance, the Derry Township supervisors will be clearly guilty of singling out Tasman and SMT and unfairly applying a double standard to the law. If this variance is not approved it will be an obvious case of condemnation without just compensation and SMT will forever pursue every legal means available to them until justice in this matter is reached."

Quarry opponents weren't sitting back on our heels, however. Just one more nail in the coffin was a scheduled public hearing to redesignate Trout Run as an exceptional value stream. The action was brought about by the request of the Blairsville Water Authority. Upgrading the stream's status from a cold water fishery to exceptional value would increase protections for the stream and the watershed.

Six people were scheduled to testify, getting five minutes each: Bradley E. Smith, SMT Family Partnership attorney; Paul Supowitz, attorney for the Chestnut Ridge Conservancy; Maggie Rosborough for the Hillside Community Association; myself, representing the Mid-Atlantic Karst Conservancy; Tom Metzgar, representing Loyalhanna Grotto and Jim Eichenlaub of the Builders Association of Metropolitan Pittsburgh.

Vic Smith Jr. told the *Tribune-Review* it was an attempt to drive "another wedge" regarding development of the ridgelands.

Smith said that quarry opponents felt it was a good idea to prevent future development by having the stream reclassified and said the family was singled out because quarry opposition wanted to use the tactic as a "wedge" to stop them.

Calling it the same old stop the quarry story, Smith said that 99 percent of the stream reclassification affected his family's property. He called it "taking someone's property and making it useless."

"They own the property," said Paul Supowicz. "But Trout Run is a waterway of the commonwealth, and it deserves to be protected... The water authority made this proposal to protect its water supply, and sure, we jumped on the bandwagon—because this is a unique area that needs to be protected."

Bradley Smith, SMT's attorney, who is not related to the family, said that "Exceptional value is basically a 'no-development' classification. At such extremely pristine criteria, there's no way there could be any kind of discharge into that watershed...and we're not talking about anything drastic, we're talking about parts-per-million."

He said it would eliminate plans for home construction, timbering, and, in a new twist, a four-seasons resort Vic Smith Jr. mentioned.

Because the entire watershed is on private property, Bradley Smith called it a condemnation.

"Who here among us wouldn't want a pristine trout stream cascading through our property, rather than scummy sewage or brown silt-laden quarry drainage?" Tom Metzgar asked. "We Loyalhanna Grotto members often encounter pristine caves relatively untouched by humans. Just as often, we find polluted, vandalized, wantonly destroyed caves, and putrid, trash filled and silted underground streams. Spoiled caves almost always suffer from one of two human foibles: ignorance, and greed. Certainly none of us in this room are ignorant of the degrading impacts we humans have had in the past and could have in the future upon Trout Run. Thus, the primary cause for future degradation of the Trout Run watershed can only stem from that ancient evil, the love of money. For us, our descendants, and for the wildlife and the Creator of all, we must preserve our little piece of Pennsylvania—the Trout Run watershed—by declaring it an exceptional value stream."

In the midst of this, in October, even before the township supervisors made their ruling on the road variance request, Tasman resources suddenly, in a one-sentence praecipe, asked Commonwealth Court to "please discontinue, withdraw and end this matter."

"I think they (Tasman) recognized that their permit was not very good," Jim Rosenberg said. "They may be thinking of starting over, or they may be going away, but I don't know."

"We really don't think that this is over," said Chestnut Ridge Conservancy President Joshua C. Whetzel III of Ligonier Township. "We hope that it is, but we really don't believe that this is just going to go away."

"Obviously, we are pleased with Tasman's decision to end this matter," commented Maggie Rosborough. "But we're also wondering what (Tasman) is up to. ... If Tasman should decide to start all over again and reapply for a new permit, we will be on our vigil and take whatever steps necessary to safeguard our community and its residents."

In spite of our skepticism, however, it was the beginning of the end.

As the quarry protest wound slowly to an end, I frequently thought of my grandfather, Albert Smith, who spent a lifetime up on Chestnut Ridge, and from whom I gained my love of it as well.

Chapter 20

Early in our quarry protest, it appeared that Tasman was assuming the role of King of the Mountain, and the bulldozers, log skidders and chainsaws were the best tools to gain that throne. But we had used eastern woodrats, bats, and underground voids to slow down the machinery. The Chestnut Ridge Conservancy had used plants, water, and quarry dust studies. And the Hillside Community Association had used decades-old deeds, pieces of paper, to stop them.

The reams of paper had piled up during all of the litigation, hearings, and appeals. So it was no real surprise that paper—the daily newspaper—would bring us news, good news. On Saturday, February 27, we woke up to see the headline in the business section of the *Tribune-Review:* "Chestnut Ridge Tract Ripe For Purchase. Sealed-Bid Auction Set For 4,500-Acre Site."

There was no rejoicing, however. It was more like apprehension. Certainly, all of the voices involved in the quarry protest had contributed to the demise of the quarry, and the exhaustion of Tasman's resources and of the property owners' patience. But those opponents and issues were well-known. With the old owners now expressing an interest in selling the property, and Tasman all but out of it, a new owner or developer could conceivably start the whole process again.

"Because of the diverse nature of the assets of this property and the differing uses of potential buyers, we feel the sealed-bid method is the fairest process for everyone concerned," Vic Smith, Jr., said in a press release announcing a sealed-bid auction via the National Real Estate Clearinghouse Inc., Chicago.

While conservation was mentioned as a potential use of the property, so was investment and development and mineral excavation.

"They feel there is a lot of potential upside to a sale, and now is the time to do it," said Adam Feldman, senior vice president of the real estate firm. The company advertised in the *Wall Street Journal,* then expanded its marketing to other newspaper ads as well as direct mail.

"We have had expressions of interest by potential buyers from all over the United States, as well as the Pennsylvania Game Commission and many local entities," Smith said. The propaganda noted that that "several timber reports indicate over six million feet of harvestable timber at this time."

They even went so far as to state that "the property provides excellent hunting and hiking and is well-suited for a private hunting and game preserve. Although not permitted at this time, the opportunity exists to develop some of the most outstanding rock climbing and caving in the area."

The sale even got Tasman and SMT clashing, as SMT filed a lawsuit in February against Tasman, declaring the lease option Tasman had tried to exercise null and void. SMT stated in the lawsuit that Tasman's option agreement "created a cloud on SMT's title to the Ridge Property" and thus hampered its attempts to market the land. The validity of the option agreement was invalid, in the minds of SMT, because Tasman failed to get the mining permit according to requirements of the previous lease agreement.

Rumors came and went, as did the months, but nothing seemed to come of any of them. So we were left to play a waiting game. But in the meantime, Tom and I finally settled the estate of my grandfather, Albert Smith, and in May of 2001 became the owners of Bear Cave, as well as some of his other real estate on Chestnut Ridge. He died November 15, 1991. The estate was complicated by a bonding issue related to a coal strip mine my grandfather had operated and was very complex. Coupled with the snail-like pace at which some attorneys work, it took nearly a decade to have it settled.

So when we finally got the deed it really seemed like the denouement of a very long drama. But our transaction was not without its own excitement. Tom and I had known that we were about to finally acquire Bear Cave since early in 2001. As the estate was finally coming to a close, our peace of mind was shattered by a letter my mother received on April 24, 2001. Let's just say that this was news ... bad news. It was from McGrath & Associates, P.C., a Greensburg law firm. It was a notice of sheriff's sale of real estate to property surrounding Bear Cave.

The property was owned by my grandfather's nephew, Don J. Smith, whose dad was my grandfather's brother, Donald. There were 400 acres. The debt was $400,000. The same notice was sent to Victor Smith, also my grandfather's brother, and the instigator of SMT Family Partnership. The reason this was so critical is that in spite of all the legal arguments and environmental issues that we brought up during our quarry protest, the only reason the Environmental Hearing Board judge gave for disapproving the quarry permit was that SMT had no access. In a nutshell, if the Don Smith property was acquired by SMT, Tasman, or a future quarry operator would have a way out. A way for their trucks to get off the ridge. A way that would take it right past Bear Cave and out Bear Cave Hollow.

We contemplated what our cave conservancy could do. We were a small group, already about $10,000 in debt while paying off our West Virginia property, with no big donor bases. If we were able to come up with a loan for the money we would have had no way to pay it back. Aside from that, family politics from many years ago caused Don to dislike SMT, as well as any other relatives. So there could be no negotiations with him. This all really hit home when we were walking to Bear Cave via Don's property and saw the stake with the sheriff's sale flyers posted in the middle of the trail. The sale was on July 2, 2001. There was no way Don would accept our help. So we had to figure out a way to make things work without actually helping on the deal, especially as we could not afford it, and personally, Tom and I were about to go into big debt to acquire the property we did.

Knowing all this it didn't take long to figure out that our only shot was with the organization best known for creation of many parks and protecting hundreds of thousands of acres in western Pennsylvania—The Western Pennsylvania Conservancy, based in Pittsburgh.

The WPC, for those not familiar with the organization, owns Fallingwater, the Frank Lloyd Wright house built on a waterfall near Ohiopyle State Park. The WPC owns the Bear Run Nature Reserve adjacent to Fallingwater, acquired much of the land of Ohiopyle State Park, Moraine State Park, and project upon project in our half of the state.

Since we had already compiled data on the area for our quarry protest, it actually took only a day for us to compile a three-page letter outlining the importance of this acquisition, and the properties adjoining it. One thing we did have going for us is that the property is adjacent to 1000-plus acres owned by the state that the state had no access for. This property would provide the access. We mailed our letter April 25. Some of the highlights noted:

"All of this information regarding a quarry proposal which was defeated may seem insignificant now, if not for two facts:

"1) Rulings were never made to defeat the quarry on all the environmental, air quality, water quality, species of concern arguments and presentations. The quarry was defeated because there was no access. Essentially, the SMT parcel adjacent to the Don J. Smith and Albert Smith estate parcels was landlocked, even at 5,000 acres.

"2) Tasman Resources owner Dan Slavek of Derry Construction Co. now has a quarry elsewhere in Derry Twp., and not on Chestnut Ridge. So now the SMT Family Partnership is shopping the limestone on its property to Amerikohl, a firm with much larger resources than Tasman, and with ready-made access to all of our arguments to fight the quarry. If the Don J. Smith property is acquired by SMT Family Partnership or Amerikohl, the access problems for the proposed quarry would be over and the threats to the ridge and its populations of threatened and endangered plants and animals will loom large.

"Acquisition of the 400 acres of property now up for Sheriff's Sale for slightly under $400,000 would:

"1) Thwart any access attempts made by SMT and help decrease the odds that a quarry operation at the crest of Chestnut Ridge is viable.

"2) Protect part of one of the largest remaining roadless areas in Westmoreland County and on Chestnut Ridge.

"3) Protect a threatened species, the eastern woodrat.

"4) Protect an endangered plant, the thick-leaved meadow-rue.

"5) Protect recently drilled backup water wells of the Blairsville Municipal Authority on the Don J. Smith property.

"6) Provide access and resolve property line disputes with the 1100 adjacent acres owned by the Commonwealth of Pennsylvania. With access and boundaries properly marked, this property can now become part of the Forbes State Forest and possibly be declared a natural area, with foot traffic access and availability for studies.

"7) Protect the Shirey Run Watershed and the Torrance State Hospital water supply, and an exceptional value stream.

"8) Protect a scenic viewshed highly visible from the Route 22 corridor."

A few days later I got a call from Melanie Moon, a vice president of the WPC, who was in charge of acquisitions. They saw the need, but didn't have a lot of time or assured funding for the acquisition.

She worked diligently on this, but the negotiations had their ups and downs. The WPC board authorized the acquisition. The State

Forest said the acquisition could be worked into a future budget. But the WPC had no short-term grants or committed donors to fund such a purchase. And it was taking a risk that if it committed its own money to the acquisition, the WPC would not be able to act on any other "emergencies" for quite some time. It was a risk worth taking.

On June 28, the Thursday before the Monday sheriff's sale, the WPC acquired the property from Don J. Smith for $400,000. The tension those past two weeks was almost palpable. I got a call from Melanie Moon the day the WPC closed. The relief was immediate. Don Smith was propelled more than anything else by a desire to see the property his father had acquired preserved. We also had the same desire. Obviously it was shared by many conservationists. Melanie told me that even John Oliver, the Pennsylvania Department of Conservation and Natural Resources (DCNR) Secretary was consulted. And he told her to acquire the property "at any cost." The Don Smith property and the 1100 acres the state owns on adjoining lands has become State Forest Land. The designation of the parcels, such as a 'wild area' or 'natural area' may not be determined for a while, and the management plan will probably take some time to develop.

We would have to wait two more years until the adjacent parcels finally left the control of the SMT Family Partnership. The property was sold in March of 2003 and is no longer in control of those who wish to deforest, mine away the ridge or permit ATVs to rip and tear all over the place. The Trout Run Woods Partnership, L.P. (TRWPLP), in the spring of 2003 finalized the purchase of lands in Westmoreland County, comprising approximately 4,000 acres and, of interest to us, 30 caves.

The members of the Trout Run Woods Limited Partnership were not unknown to us. They had been active supporters and participants in the Chestnut Ridge Conservancy's efforts against the quarry, and, as adjacent property owners on the Fairfield Township side of the ridge, had even filed suit against Tasman for potential illegal water discharge onto their property. Bob Eppley and I had seen partner David Shapira testify during the Environmental Hearing Board hearing in Judge Renwand's chambers. His story of how his family began going to Chestnut Ridge, their appreciation for nature, and the huge amount of time they spent working on and enjoying their property left no doubt in my mind that this family loved the ridge and that nothing would ever threaten it again.

As the snow melted, we began extending our walks on the tram road along the reservoir beyond the property boundary where I had had to turn around once the Smiths forbade me to use their property. I began emailing and talking to Edie Shapira, another one of the Trout Run Woods Partners, and Tom and I arranged to meet her one warm day in the meadow at the top of the ridge. Aside from three site visits, it had been almost a decade since I had been able to visit the ridge and not worry about logging, or mining, or bulldozers, or being caught trespassing. We were about to start one of many adventures with Edie, all of us anxious to share old secrets about the ridge, make new discoveries, and do all we could to help the new landowners work to bring back the ridge we all remembered and loved so well.

As we got out of my Jeep at the meadow, pulling over along Tasman's intended quarry road, I spotted traces of the old path we used to follow past the old school bus hunting camp. It was still there. So were we.

Tom Metzgar, left, Neal Krause, at top, and Dennis Melko, below, removing the gate from Con Cave after it was all over. Our conservancy, the Mid-Atlantic Karst Conservancy, Inc., leased the cave from the new owners and it is open, with permission, to responsible cavers. The MAKC now manages caves on the Trout Run Woods Preserve.

Neal Krause entering Copperhead Cave after the property changed hands. The MAKC now manages caves on the Trout Run Woods Preserve on behalf of the owners. For information visit www.karst.org.